you're doing it wrong

josh gunderson

First edition.

The characteristics of some individuals and chronology of some events have been changed.

Author Photos: Monica Poulin

ISBN: 978-1-7956-1666-9

contents

I am here, I am here
I've already seen the bottom,
so there's nothing to fear,
I know that I'll be ready,
when the devil is near
-P!NK, *I Am Here*

enter the circus

Hello and welcome to my book!

I have always wanted to be a writer. As long as I can remember, it's all I really wanted to do. I've had, and still do have, a lot of other dreams, but writing has been the number one for quite some time. From the days of elementary school and beyond I have always been writing something. In my early years it was funny, weird little stories. I really wish I still had some of them because I remember they were quite ridiculous.

Remember those fluff pens that Cher used in the movie Clueless? I wrote a three part series about evil fluff pens from space that were trying to take over the world, starting with Sewell-Anderson Elementary school. If that's not a New York Times best-seller then I really don't know what is. Sadly, there are no known copies of these stories.

In high school I went through my angsty poetry phase. Those were some emo gold. Those I still have! Matter of fact, for my senior year project in high school I wrote a collection of painfully depressing essays and poems. I compiled them together in a book called "Reflections" which, as far as I know, there is only one surviving copy and it will never again see the light of day. It currently lives in my underwear drawer.

In college I went through the Creative Writing concentration. I wrote short plays and began mapping out ideas for different book series and so much more. I still have all of these somewhere, who knows what will become of them. As time went on, I never lost sight of my dream despite seeming to never have time for it.

Growing up sucks.

But no matter where life took me, there was always this nagging desire to do something. To write something. To tell a story and share something special and unique with the world. But what?

"You should totally write a book" was a common refrain from friends, family, and even complete strangers. While speaking at schools and community events I am constantly asked if I'd ever thought of putting together some of my stories and releasing a book.

An interesting thought.

Why haven't I done that? I consider myself a storyteller. When people ask what I do for a living, that's what I tell them. I tell stories. So when it came to writing a book it only makes sense that the first story I share with the world is mine.

Now, most people are of the belief that memoirs are only interesting when they come from celebrities or politicians- people who had lived insane lives in the public eye and want to make some extra money by telling the story behind the story. Lurid tales of movie sets and Hollywood scandal. Politicians and whatever it is that they do. These are the stories people want to hear.

But what about mine? Would anyone be interested in knowing about me? My rise to fame too young and too fast leading me to mental breakdown only to reemerge as the queen of pop? Okay, that might be Britney Spears but don't tell me that I can't write a memoir just because I'm not world famous. I mean, when you really break it down I'm the most famous person currently sitting in my living room. The point is that I don't like people telling me what I can't do.

At one point, in my late twenties, I was travelling to Florida a lot. I went Walt Disney World for the first time in 2011 at the ripe old age of 25 and I was hooked

3

instantly. From there I was making regular treks down from Boston to visit the Most Magical Place on Earth.

Real quick side note. Walt Disney World is billed as the Most Magical Place on Earth. Disneyland, in California, is the Happiest Place on Earth. I can't even begin to describe how insanely upset I get when people confuse the two. Get it right people. Get it right or I will cut you.

"Josh, you have to be an adult, you can't just live at Disney," my office-mate told me one day.

Challenge. Fucking. Accepted.

In 2014 I packed up my cats and everything I owned and made the horrendous drive from Boston to Orlando. Before my first box was unpacked I was at the front gates of the Magic Kingdom buying my annual pass. I haven't looked back since.

Don't tell me what I can't do.

So maybe I'm not a celebrity or politician but I am a guy with a story to tell. My delusions of grandeur know no bounds. That and I've totally got a plan.

Step 1: Write Book

Step 2: Sell lots of said book

Step 3: Be awesome

The hardest part of all of these steps was definitely the first one. Granted, once I've finally finished that step there's the challenge of the second but let's take this one at a time, okay? At this point in the writing process, I have been on this earth for thirty years. I can't even come close to claiming that I know everything to know about life. Not by a long shot.

I've come to learn that at thirty years old, my life is just really beginning. There's just one very simple problem: I have no idea what I'm doing.

When the idea for this book first came about ten years ago I was going through what my friend Jo called my "quarter life crisis." I was constantly freaking out about what I was doing with my life and what the point of it all was. Instead of running off to join a cult I decided to ponder exactly what I was going through and what it means to be having this type of life crisis. I knew I was too young and broke for hookers and a sports car so this was going to require some problem-solving skills and deep meditation.

Or margaritas with my sister.

For the record, I'm just assuming that the above is how cults are born. A group of twenty-something's that feel their lives are going nowhere and rather than dealing with it they run away and eventually find one another and from there find something to worship that they think will make their lives better. Like the Kardashians.

From all of this, the idea for this book was born and while, over the past ten years, so much of the content has changed, the theme has always remained the same. I have no idea what the hell I'm doing.

What follows in these many pages are the little nuggets of wisdom that I have discovered from living my life and the many existential crisis's I have experienced in that time. Perhaps you can find some insight for yourself.

If anything you can have a good laugh at my misfortune. You're welcome.

Or, if you don't want to read this whole book but you still want to impress your book club, there's only one thing you need to know about life:

You're doing it wrong.

look what you made me do

I will never pretend that I am a perfect person. I've had to remind people constantly that I am, indeed, a human being. Flawed by nature. Flawed by circumstance. Flawed.

What follows on these pages is my version of the truth. These are the stories of my life as I remember them happening and therefore may be inherently different from how the people involved in the same moments remember them. There's a good chance those same people might not particularly enjoy what I have to say about them. Two sides to every story and whatnot.

Perspective.

In an effort to provide these people with some semblance of plausible deniability, I have altered some of the details in these stories. Sometimes I've changed names, other times it's dates, others it's locations. All of this in an effort to make less savory people feel better about themselves. They can discuss this book with their friends, having read stories of their own wrongdoings and be able to say, "I can't believe anyone would do that do another person, how disgraceful."

"I agree, people can be real scum sometimes," their friends will say, highlighting specific moments of particular douchbaggery.

"I would never do something like that!" They say with an air of superiority reserved only for those deep in denial about what is real versus the picture perfect self they have created in their minds.

You're welcome for this by the way.

Look at the good I do.

But then I can't help but think about what this all really means. I mean, I've changed the names and other pertinent details but what has that really accomplished?

If you are a random person who happened to pick this book up and started reading (thanks for that!), there's a good chance that you're not going to know who I am and by extension won't have a clue who I am talking about. However, let's say we worked together, or went to school together, dated, or whatever- you're probably going to know someone in this book. Hell, you might be one of those people. Rather than getting mad at me for telling tales- enjoy the ride. You're famous! Though I changed your name.

Life's a bitch.

Other names I have not changed because I have nothing but nice things to say about these people and I'm really hopeful that they're not going to sue me.

Nina, please don't sue me.

JOSH GUNDERSON

everybody poops

It is an unfortunate, but true, aspect of life that we spend an absurd amount of time comparing ourselves to others. Whether we like it or not, we are constantly, mentally, sizing one another up in an effort to see who has it better.

With the advent of social media this has gotten so much worse. I'll fully admit there are times that I have logged on, scrolled through my news feed and promptly closed my laptop to go raid the fridge in an effort to eat my feelings.

It always seems like everyone who isn't me is out having the time of their lives, living every moment to the fullest. People are at the beach, at the club, singing karaoke all while I'm at home alone, holding a Netflix marathon of 30 Rock while surrounded by more than one cat and more than one empty bottle of wine.

Through it all there is one simple fact that keeps me smiling, keeps me going, and most importantly keeps me sane:

Everybody poops.

It is this one simple fact that you really just can't ignore. From rock stars to presidents, a-listers to Kathy Griffin, the highest ranking CEO to the guy in the mailroom.

We all poop.

So there's something to keep in mind next time the high school quarterback gives you are hard time or your boss is endlessly screaming at you. Try not to smile too much as you remember that they too have had a bad trip to Taco Bell that left them with that uncomfortable shift in their intestines and that knowing feeling that there will be repeated trips to the bathroom to evacuate the dance floor.

We may not talk about it, but we all know it happens.

The one big exception to this would be runners. Runners are obsessed with poop. We talk about it constantly. Don't believe me? Find yourself a runner and strike up a conversation about their last race. I can promise you they will have something to say about poop somewhere along the line.

I guess what I'm trying to get at is that we are all human beings. None of us are perfect and we shouldn't always believe what we see in front of us, especially when it comes to social media. We all want to impress one another. No one's going to advertise the bad things, we're going to focus on and share the good stuff.

While I was working at the aquarium in Boston I had taken a position as a supervisor in the box office and found myself diving quite deeply into this very topic with one of my staffers, Justin. He wasn't having the greatest day and came into my office where he proceeded to have a complete and utter mental breakdown.

Let me pause here to mention that there is nothing wrong with a good old-fashioned meltdown. If there is one thing that I absolutely love, it's opening a nice bottle of wine, popping in a depressing movie about lost love, dead animals or anything involving war, and having a good old-fashion, ugly snot-cry.

You know the one.

There are just tears and snot everywhere and you wipe it away with your sleeve because you just don't care anymore.

Also there's wine.

The great catharsis that comes from this night of drunken crying is nothing short of wonderful.

But I digress.

I didn't have any wine for Justin and I feel like it probably would have been a violation of some sort of policy to give alcohol to one of my employees while we were both on the clock and in my office. Though I have always wanted to be one of those guys that had a full bar in his office to sip on whiskey and look wistfully out the window thinking about how rich I was. My office in the aquarium actually didn't have a window so that plan was out for the time being.

During his breakdown, Justin went on to say many of the things I had been feeling years before. He felt like he was falling behind everyone else in life. He had gone to community college and received his associates degree while others in his life had received their bachelors or beyond. He talked about the frustrations of seeing his friends getting married, buying houses and having kids all while he was feeling stuck.

Sound familiar?

The truth is, in that moment, despite our age difference and that fact that I was his superior, Justin and I were having the same feelings towards life. Two of my friends had just gotten engaged, another friend was on his second kid, and my younger sister had just gotten married.

Sure, from the outside looking in, my life looked pretty awesome. On Facebook I'm charming and whitty and living the Life of Riley. My Instagram account shows off my grand adventures and the madness of someone who spends an obscene amount of time in theme parks. At work I'm calm, collected and seem to know exactly what I'm doing.

On the inside? I'm screaming like a lost child in a K-Mart. It's all an act and I told Justin as much. That's the reality of the world. We're all a little scared and frankly, don't have a clue what we're doing. We're just too proud to admit it. That's the honest to God truth.

Everybody poops.

cleanin' out my closet

"If you untie your belly button, your butt will fall off!" This was my mom's favorite thing to tell us when we were kids and for the life of me, I have no idea why. The sad part is that we totally believed her. She's a nurse and we really had no choice but to take her word for it.

I now know that there is no link between my belly button and my butt. Also you can't untie a bellybutton. On that same vein I still get nervous when I am mining for lint because I can't afford to have less butt than I already have.

It's so funny how much we take on blind faith when we are young. We trust that the adults in our lives have some idea what is going on. They are older and wiser and have jobs and checkbooks and know how to pay bills. Adults rule the world. As kids, we long for the days where we can feel that same amazing power and know all the amazing things that they know.

Like basic human anatomy.

Then you start to get older. Your teenage years slowly melt into your twenties and then the next thing you know, you're thirty. Worst of all, during all of that you're in a constant state of panic because you have no flipping idea what the hell is going on. You know nothing. You find yourself just making it all up as you go along and hoping no one calls you on it. Little do you know, everyone else is doing the exact same thing. I can personally testify that roughly 90% of my adult life has been spent on Google trying to figure out how to do stuff.

Hand to heart- I do it all the time.

There is never a day when you wake up and a switch has been flipped and suddenly you are imparted with a world of knowledge and experience and are finally an amazing adult. Sure, there are some moments when you find yourself feeling pretty grown up but those are few and far between when it comes down to it. They come at the strangest times, when you really don't expect it.

For me, one such moment came during my friend Pete's 30th birthday party. His daughter and the other kids were playing all over the house and in the backyard while the moms of the group were keeping a close eye while also playing video games in the living room. Most of the guys had gathered in the kitchen.

We were all standing in a circle talking about nothing of extreme consequence, just a bunch of guys with beer, shooting the shit. I happened to catch one of the kids at the party looking over at our little group in the kitchen. He sat there, quiet in the moment, just observing the bunch of us talking and laughing.

I remembered being the same way when I was younger and living with my dad. He worked at an auto shop and every day at quitting time he and the guys would do a beer run at the liquor store across the street and hang out swapping stories in the now quiet shop. I would find myself sitting on the outskirts of these powwows, an outsider, too young to take part in what was clearly an adult moment.

Now here I was finally a part of that moment. It wasn't anything special, just a bunch of grown men having an in depth conversation about Star Wars and Marvel movies. However, truth be told, I felt like a bona fide grown up. The problem is just how few and far between these moments are and they never seem to show up when I really need them. For every moment that I feel like I might have a grip on what's going on, ten new ones show up where I feel clueless.

Was I ever going to get this thing right? Does anyone? Maybe some people do. Either that or they're just get really great at pretending they have an idea as to what the hell is going on but in reality they are just as lost. I discovered this was the truth with the more "adult" people in my life.

In the spring of 2013 I was hired to speak at a tech conference in Hawaii. This was my first time visiting the islands and I felt like it was something I shouldn't be experiencing alone so I invited my mom along to join me. One night while at dinner the conversation turned from how breathtaking Hawaii is to talk of general on-goings in life. I shared with my mom some of the conversations my older sister and I seemed to be having over and over again about our journey into adulthood. At this point the two of us were nearing our 30's and were casually freaking out over how behind we both felt.

We both had friends who were getting married, having kids and buying houses and here we were both single, renting and walking that fine line that divides the normal people from the crazy cat ladies.

It was my turn to feel lost and desolate. How could I be so behind? At this point in my life I had been running my own business for about five years, living on my own, and had a pretty decent life. There it was. I was 28 years old and still feeling like a lost teenager. Hell, here I was, sitting on a tropical island, drinking some sort of delicious, fruity alcoholic beverage and I had my own checkbook!

What am I doing wrong?

"Don't look at me," my mom said over her own cocktail. "I still don't have a clue what the hell I'm doing."

There is was. With that single statement my worldview shifted in an entirely new direction. For so long I thought that I was just royally screwing everything up. That I was going about life in the completely wrong way. The truth of the matter was that I was letting the world lead me to believe that I was doing everything wrong.

One of the most important life lessons that no one will tell you is that it's okay to be clueless sometimes. It's perfectly acceptable to make mistakes. To stumble. To fall. It's okay to fail.

Sure, it really sucks to go into a situation and come out the other end having failed miserably but it's what we do with that failure that really defines who we are. It's all a part of the growing process and that's the other truth of life right there. We are never done learning and growing.

There is no instruction manual or college course for adulthood that will explain how the world works. We learn it all through our own trial and error and, believe me, there will be plenty of errors. It's how we chose to move forward from each bump in the road.

In life we learn a lot of interesting lessons along the way and it's up to us to either recognize those lessons or ignore them. A lot of the time we're too busy being wrapped up in our problems that we don't notice there is some great wisdom being bestowed upon us until it's too late.

Grow from these lessons.

Some people will embrace the world around them and chose to live in these moments of great wisdom and grow from them. Others will live in fear of reality and fear causes people to do some pretty stupid things.

What follows now is my own journey, written in the hopes that there are lessons to be learned from my own little bumps in the road. Know that I've done the best I could and still am trying my hardest every day to learn and grow.

I also completely realize that at this point I have introduced this book four different times and I am totally procrastinating getting things going.

Why?

First, I'm absolutely terrified. I have no idea where this journey is going to take me. There are parts of me and my life that I'd really rather forget about but I know that to omit them would be doing myself a great disservice. There are a great many things in the pages to follow that I had chosen to forget over time but have come raging forward in my mind as I've explored some of my past, pain demanding to be felt, reality demanding to be seen.

Second, I have no idea what I am doing. There are no instruction manuals on how to write the story of your life. That's a lie. There are. You can buy them on Amazon and they are a complete waste of money. Or so I've heard from a friend.

That friend is me.

Anyone who has written a book can tell you that it is the hardest damn thing you will ever do. More so when you are writing your own story because it can sometimes be the hardest story to tell.

Also, speaking from experience, you will drink a lot of wine while writing a book and this can be both helpful and hurtful. Nothing spells a good time like drunkenly digging up repressed memories of childhood trauma!

I do it for the art really.

You're also going to nap a lot while writing a book because you're exhausted from all the sitting and typing. Also, the childhood memories.

And the wine.

What follows has been almost a decade in the making and has gone through more changes than I can count.

But isn't that what life is?

I'm really asking because I don't have a clue.

Here we go.

superheroes

My story begins on a high school field trip where I was bitten by a radioactive spider while being exposed to harmful gamma rays after being selected by the US Government for a super soldier program, which resulted in my becoming the God of Thunder.

And that was all during kindergarten!

As it turns out, I came into this world already establishing myself as someone who can't do anything right. I couldn't even be born properly. Unlike most people, I was not born. Instead, I was removed from my mother (not unlike a tumor) by cesarean on May 15th of 1985 at Cedar Sianai Hospital.

It is not lost on me that many celebrities have come and gone from rehab at this hospital since that time which all but guaranteed the fame that I would gain later in life (mostly all in my head). I think this parasite-like removal set me down a path to do just about everything wrong. Well, society would call it wrong, I call it being an individual. We're all beautiful and unique snowflakes. I'm just a yellow one.

My older sister, Shannon, saw this very early on and tried her damndest to fix the problem as soon as possible.

It goes without saying that her favorite story from the early days of my existence is her telling our mom to "throw her precious little baby in the trash." So much so that if I didn't include that little tidbit somewhere in this book she would probably never speak to me again. I have no idea why I feel that way, but she would be pissed and I would certainly hear about it.

Despite Shannon's best efforts, I managed to stick around to make her life miserable. Turns out I gave her a sense of purpose as she more often than not was there to save me from myself.

My earliest memory of doing it wrong comes from sometime in the third grade where I took the game to a whole new level. While shopping at K-Mart I happened upon an amazing pair of Mighty Morphin Power Rangers shorts. As the Power Rangers were the new talk of the town (step aside Teenage Mutant Ninja Turtles) I was quite keen to own them. My mom obliged and I was set to be the coolest kid at school come Monday morning.

One small problem.

They were boxer shorts.

They were boxer shorts and I wore them with the ignorant pride of a third grade moron. Thankfully, third graders in the mid-nineties weren't all that bright and no one seemed to notice my fashion faux pas or if they did, they were nice enough not to mention it. The latter seems unlikely simply because no one seemed to have a problem pointing out what a loser I was.

There was one time that same year where the school was having a clash day. The point was to intentionally wear clothes that didn't match. Upon hearing the announcement one boy in my class commented, "maybe that'll be the day Josh's clothes match for once."

He laughed. I laughed. We all laughed.

Well, I laughed until I realized he was talking about me. Mid-nineties third graders are jerks.

Most of my early years were spent in the city of Atascadero, California which is best known for being the setting of the novel turned movie starring a young Haley Joel Osment, Pay it Forward. Well, the novel took place in Atascadero where the movie took place in

Las Vegas so that Helen Hunt could be a stripper or something.

Growing up, we always had animals in our family. Our pets at any given point in time included cats, rats, dogs, horses and even a potbellied pig named Wally who later grew to be roughly the size of a Volkswagen Beatle.

I honestly believe that growing up taking care of so many animals was pivotal in how my siblings and I developed. Maybe more so for Shannon and I since my younger brother and sister, Erik and Melinda, didn't get as much of that redneck life as we did. That might be a lie, I'm sure there's a picture of Erik somewhere in a full cowboy getup and he would kill me if I ever shared it.

Regardless, it shaped who we were and who we became later on in life. It taught us compassion, discipline, responsibility and how to look good in cowboy boots while shoveling horse poop. It might also explain why I now live with three rescue cats and tear up at even the thought of those damn Sarah McLaughlin commercials.

Damn you Sarah McLaughlin.

When it came to my family life, as far as I knew, we were fairly normal. I don't know if I was just young and naïve or my parents did a decent job of covering up the truth of what was bubbling beneath the surface of their marriage.

We did the normal family things. The highlight of life was always trips to our favorite restaurant Players Pizza. My heart broke the day I found out they went out of business. It wasn't anything special but it was our favorite. We would always request the booth in the back corner where there hung a painting of a tomato sitting in an armchair. It wasn't a cartoon tomato with a face and limbs, not at all. Just a normal, red tomato sitting in an armchair.

We loved that painting.

At one point, before the restaurant closed, I called and offered to buy the painting but the manager thought I was a lunatic and hung up on me.

Weekend nights we would head to Henry's the local video store. This is a concept that I know is sadly lost on so many with the advent of Netflix and RedBox. This was even a time before Blockbuster video was even a big thing. We'd find the movie we wanted to rent on the shelves. Beneath each box was a hook with a tag on it. If the tag was there, that meant the video was available to rent. You'd take the tag to the counter where the clerk would exchange it for the VHS tape.

We were old school.

We were pretty abnormal, at times, as well. One of Shannon's favorite anecdotes of our childhood involved losing teeth. As a kid, her two front teeth (the buckteeth if you will) had grown in fused together. As time went on they, naturally, became loose.

She was pumped.

Two teeth for the price of one? The Tooth Fairy was surely going to make it rain.

We were roughhousing in the backyard one evening and I managed to deliver a firm elbow directly to Shannon's face causing the fused teeth to become fully dislodged.

She swallowed them.

She was pissed.

I can still see her sitting on the swing set crying as overly dramatic amounts of blood and snot-drool were running down her face. I'm talking hard-core ugly crying. Seriously, I want you to envision the ugliest crying you've ever seen, dial that up to eleven, add in some blood and snot-drool and there you have it.

Childhood memories.

Shannon was beyond upset at the thought of losing the payday on these teeth and from here, there was only one logical place to go because, as we all know, what goes in has to come out.

You see where this is going, right?

If you're thinking that my dad spent the better part of the next few days sifting through my sister's shit in hopes of finding the magical fused buckteeth then you are absolutely right.

Where's that Normal Rockwell painting?

Spoiler alert: he never found them.

With all this normality, I never realized that something wasn't right. Even when my parents separated, I had no idea what was going on other than my mom had moved out.

Life continued as normal.

Every Saturday morning my dad and I would wake up early and head out to the shooting range with his rifle. This was always something I'd look forward to because it was "just us guys." We'd be up before the sun and head out to a makeshift shooting range in the middle of nowhere on a road somewhere between Atascadero and Paso Robles. Sometimes we'd bring homemade targets, others we'd shoot at cans, bottles and other assorted trash that people would leave behind.

On the way home we'd stop for breakfast at this small diner that was on the way. We'd have a hearty meal of eggs, bacon, toast and pancakes. "A man's meal" my dad would call it. We'd drag ourselves back to my dad's 1957 Chevy pickup and make our way home, usually blasting the Traveling Wilburys.

There was nothing in this world that Shannon and I loved more than riding in that pickup listening to the Wilburys. Our favorite song had to be "Tweeter and the Monkey Man. Clearly we had no idea the song was about a young man who was hard up for cash so he stayed up all night with the monkey man selling cocaine and hash to an undercover cop who had a sister named Jan who also happened to be in love with the Monkey Man.

Not a clue.

We pretty much thought the song was about a guy with a pet monkey. We mostly liked it because of the line "and the walls came down, all the way to hell." We were allowed to swear and totally get away with it.

Rebels without a clue.

As it would turn out, there were a great many things that I was clueless about in the time surrounding my parent's divorce. It wasn't until two decades later, in conversations with both Shannon and a therapist that I came to grips of the reality of my childhood. The end result from those mental walls coming down was a massive purge of emotions and a trip to hell and back.

Maybe the Wilburys were on to something.

I've said it before though, I'm an advocate for a good, ugly snot-cry every now and again.

If you'll excuse me a moment.

Not too long after the divorce, my mom decided that she wanted to be closer to her family back in Massachusetts so, in the summer of 1994, we pack up our lives and said goodbye to the horses, the pig and everyone we knew to head east.

We moved to the city of Lynn, Massachusetts which anyone will be quick to point out as "Lynn, Lynn, city of sin." If you don't believe me go anywhere in the state of Massachusetts and tell someone you're from Lynn. They will pull that little limerick out so fast your head will spin.

We spent the better part of that summer living with my aunt and uncle and their three kids. It was during this time that I discovered that crazy people do exist and I am related to them.

A lot of insanity went on during those summer months but for some reason the one big bit of madness that I remember from that time was that no one was allowed to take a shower.

You read that correctly.

If you wanted to be clean in that house, you'd get that way by taking a bath and nothing else. It quickly became very clear to me that I would not be getting along with anyone in this family which was strange to because I had always gotten on well with my mom's other sister, Jody and my cousins Jayme and Joelle.

This was not the case with the Lynn side of the family. Especially my Aunt Darlene who, to this day, is one of the most ridiculously horrid people I have ever met in my life. Every Halloween she would dress as a witch to hand out candy and I saw this as less of a costume and more of her natural state.

My mom ultimately bought the house right next door to the lunatic asylum that was my aunt's home and we settled into our lives.

In the years that I lived in Lynn I started to suffer extreme bouts of depression that would manifest in some often destructive ways. I became a bit of a fire bug during this time and was obsessed with setting things on fire. I had gone through a kleptomania phase while we were still in California but I had apparently evolved my ways to pyromania. I may be a serial killer by time this comes out so we have that to look forward to.

The hardest part during all of this was losing the bond I shared with Shannon. She got along well with our cousins where I couldn't stand to be in the same room as them. We drifted apart which killed me. We had always been so close as kids and that just wasn't the case anymore. Sure we fought with each other but that never stopped us from performing killer duets of "A Whole New World" from Aladdin whenever the opportunity arose.

In leaving the world we had known in California and settling into life in Massachusetts, Shannon found a whole new side of herself that didn't involve me. Sure, I had made some great friends at school but I had lost the one consistent person that had been around as long as I could remember. Sure, she wanted to throw me in the trash can but that's what siblings do. I knocked her teeth out and made her snot cry. It's the circle of life.

When fire lost its appeal, food became my new obsession. Specifically spaghetti. I was notorious for cooking an entire package of spaghetti noodles and eating them in one sitting, usually in front of the TV. Food had become my new outlet and best friend. In no time at all I had blown up like a balloon and became a walking stereotype for American youth. Michelle Obama would not have approved.

My cousins, along with my aunt, would constantly make fun of me for my weight. Darlene was the worst of them all. She was a big fan of emotional and verbal abuse and I was her favorite target outside of her own children. She was a mess and one of the most childish people I had ever met.

This never changed.

The last time I saw her was during my grandmother's wake in the winter of 2011. We were all very positive that she was not going to show up at all as she had been a no-show at my grandfather's funeral nearly a decade prior.

I was in the sitting room with my Aunt Jody and some assorted other family members when an unfamiliar face popped in and out of the doorway.

"Who was that," Jody asked of her own sister.

I shrugged my shoulders and almost immediately we heard, "don't you fucking touch me," being screamed in the next room.

"Holy shit, it's Darlene."

What followed was ten minutes of pure chaos. There was fighting, screaming, swearing and so much more. First she got into it with my mom before storming out of the funeral home where she came face to face with my uncle, her brother. I honestly can't think of a single reality show brawl that could top anything that happened in these moments. It really would have made for great television though, we were giving the Osbournes a pretty good run for their money.

Following the screaming match with my uncle she continued towards her car where she confused Erik for her younger son. To this day, I don't have a clue what she said to him but it didn't really end well for anyone involved.

It also really doesn't help that most of the family had been drinking since dawn.

I was mortified by everything that was going on around me. The services were being held just down the street from the grocery store where I had worked through all of high school and college in a town where just about everyone knew me. This included the people living in the houses around the funeral home. The same people peaking out their windows or standing on their front porches wondering what the hell was going on.

I elected to take myself on a nice walk as far away from these on goings as possible during which I called my friend Maggie simply to vent and process the madness.

"I wonder if it's too late to get a camera crew here," I mused on the verge of my own nervous breakdown. "No one's going to believe this."

I imagine this was truly the last time I would ever see Darlene. I'm okay with this.

It did reach the point back in Lynn all those years prior where I had reached my limit with the abuse coming from Darlene and her family. Imagine scenes similar to the funeral played out on an almost daily basis.

My mom had reached her breaking point as well. I was going through puberty and I was far from being a good kid. I lied, I cheated and I stole. I was a miserable brat. One day, in the summer of 1997, she and I had a blow-out fight during which I told her I didn't want to live with her anymore. Following this, she sent me back to California to live with my dad.

daddy's little defect

It would be far too dramatic to say that life got worse after I moved back to California but it would be a lie to say that things were better. It was different. Not better. Not worse. Different.

If you aren't a child of divorce then it may be hard to understand the subtle battle that takes place for your affection. It's an ongoing performance put on by your parents of doing everything they can to be the lesser of the two evils in your eyes. Looking back on it now it's almost comical. More so in the fact that, in some ways, this little battle still continues into adulthood if you're paying enough attention.

My dad had the advantage in this little war as we lived with our mom full time on the opposite side of the country so when we made our yearly visit to him it was as if we had been transported to a whole new world. In the week that he had us there was nothing but fun and games.

It was all an act, a farce, a show to be sure. It's so easy to be the awesome parent when you only have to do it one week out of the year. There were trips to Disneyland, hiking, fishing, you name it. Life with dad was the absolute best!

That was the mindset I had when I got into that blow out fight with my mom. It's only fair to mention that it came almost immediately following one of these trips back to California for our yearly visit. I wanted to go back to that life of fun and games full-time.

So off I went.

Since the divorce, my dad had settled into life with his girlfriend. I call her that because, to this day, I'm fairly certain they're not actually married. California doesn't recognize common law marriage so I'm not sure what the hell their relationship is. I've always referred to her as my step-mom just because it was easier than trying to explain it. I find that to be the case with just about everything involving my family.

We defy explanation.

Like, real question. When my mom divorced my step-dad, what does that make him? Is there a name for it? Like, ex-step-dad? I'm sure I could search that somewhere. Is there a website for that? I'm sure there is.

Moving on.

The two had moved from Atascadero and settled in to the small seaside town of Cayucos, California. For the record, as far as I know, Cayucos has zero claim to fame though it was designated as one of the "Coolest Small Towns In America" by someone who clearly didn't live there.

I all to quickly learned that the grass had appeared so much greener on the other side. The facade of the perfect parent wore out quickly and my father's true colors shown through sooner rather than later. He didn't need to act anymore.

I can easily pinpoint the moment when I lost all respect for my father. I can't remember the exact day, time or even what year it was but the moment itself is crystal clear in my mind. He was sitting at his desk paying bills. We had been talking about nothing of consequence when I had commented on never receiving birthdays cards from him following our move to Massachusetts.

"You guys never sent me a card on my birthday so why should I send them to you?"

Direct and to the point and easily the most imma-ture thing a grown man could have said to his child.

While there were so many moments like this be-tween us in the time that I lived with him, it was in this one that a wedge was placed into our relationship which only served to separate us more and more as time went on. To this day I still can't fathom how im-mature you have to be to say something like that to your child, to feel that way.

He did have our birthdays marked in his planner though. The sole purpose was to count down until each of us had turned 18 years old. The day he no longer had to pay child support for us. He told me as much as often as possible. It was a joke to him. We were his kids but he looked at us as more of a burden than family.

It was also during this time that I became fully aware of my father's alcoholism. It had always been there but I was just too young and blind to see it. Now it played out in full force in front of me every single day. Looking back now on that time, knowing how he drank, it's actually quite astonishing to me that I am still alive.

My dad would start drinking from the moment his work day ended and would continue until he went to bed. It was not uncommon to find empty beer cans in the shower. His favorite trick was taking the wrapper off of a soda bottle and putting it around a beer can so that he could drink and drive with no one the wiser.

One Thanksgiving when we were making the drive to northern California to my uncle's house, he drank the whole way, most of the time not even hiding it. There was a full cooler in the car when we started our trip that would be emptied long before we completed the seven hour drive.

Seriously, a wonder I'm alive.

It is almost impossible to count the number of times that he would put my life at risk because of his drinking.

One of the scariest instances came the day of the annual Cayucos Car Show. My dad was the head of the show and for this particular year he had secured a beer truck for the event. Following the day's event the kegs were still pretty full and my dad and his friends enjoyed the seemingly endless supply of free beer.

In retrospect it would have been a smart idea to just walk myself home. We only lived about three miles or so from town and the walk wasn't all that bad. At the same time, I was overweight and lazy so it was just easier to stick around and watch a bunch of grown men get increasingly intoxicated.

The time finally came when the kegs were tapped out and the party was over. Before we made our way home my dad stopped at the liquor store for a six pack. Ever the amazing actor, he made it out with his bounty, the clerk never once questioning his sobriety or lack thereof.

We began the terrifying drive home in that same 1957 Chevy that I had loved spending time in as a kid.

It was quickly clear, only to me apparently, that the man should not have been behind the wheel of a motor vehicle as he spent more time in just about every lane besides the one he wanted. The truck has a manual transmission and this was proving tricky for him to operate in his condition. His condition being that of a drunken man with the steering wheel in one hand and an open beer in the other.

There is a red light along the way and at this point we were to be, mercifully, turning off the highway here and onto the road that would lead us home. The light turned green and my dad, hand full of steering wheel and beer, yelled at me to shift the gear for him. I didn't have the slightest clue what I was supposed to do and just sat frozen in my seat.

There was a lot of confusion, yelling and a spilt beer. And then he hit me.

We sat on the side of the road, him cleaning up the mess of beer and me, sitting shocked and silent as I did my best to hold back tears. That was the first time he had ever done anything like that but it wouldn't be the last. The can of worms had been opened.

It took me a long time to realize just how weak my father was. He could never stand up to my step-mom who was clearly the dominant member of the house. She was controlling, mean-tempered and every bit as abusive as he was. He couldn't stand up to her so he took his frustrations out on me.

For the longest time I blamed his behavior on the alcohol. It was the only thing that made sense through it all. I also spent a great deal of time blaming myself. I became quite adept at lying during all of this. You have to when the cuts and bruises get noticed. I sunk into a deep depression and continued to self-medicate with food. That wedge between my father and me pushed us further and further apart and I became reclusive. I would spend hours, sometimes days locked away in my room in an effort to just be invisible. Weekends were usually the worst because from breakfast to dinner he had a beer in his hand.

Sometime in 8th grade the lies began to get harder and harder to tell. It was my gym teacher that first noticed something was wrong during a trip to the local pool as a part of class. She had asked about a bruise and I gave her the company line.

Soon enough I was getting pulled out of class regularly to meet with a woman I had never seen before. It honestly didn't dawn on my until many years later that the school had called child protective services. I would be called out of class to meet with her in a dark office. The conversations were always the same.

"How are things at home?"

"Fine." A lie.

"How are you getting along with your step-mother?"

"Fine." A lie.

"And your father?"

A lie.

"How did you get the bruises on your legs?"

A lie.

These little meetings went on for the better part of a month. No action was ever taken because I never came clean about what was happening at home. I was scared but, more than that, I was ashamed. I couldn't stand up for myself and was too afraid to say something. I was afraid of the consequences if he ever found out I had said anything. But he did find out.

During the investigation they had gotten in contact with my dad. I don't know what was said on that end of things but I know he was livid. He came into my room one night, wasted beyond belief, and began screaming, throwing things, and hitting.

I was told under no uncertain terms was I to talk about anything that happened at home with anyone. It wasn't anybody else's business and I was to keep my mouth shut or pay the price. I kept my mouth shut and my head down. Eventually the investigation was dropped. If I was unwilling to say anything, why bother continuing. I stuck to my stories behind the bruises and they had no choice but to take it as the truth.

Then in 2000 I was offered the choice to move back to Massachusetts. I had gone back that summer to visit and had been convinced to make the move by my soon to be step-father Henry. It didn't take much to sell me on the idea of coming home.

The grass is always greener.

The last time I saw my dad was the day he dropped me off at the airport. He had walked me to the gate and stayed with me until boarding had begun. Not much conversation took place but I do remember the last moment we had together. The announcement came for boarding and the time had come to leave. He reached his hand out to me and said, "Good luck son."

It was one of those moments you think only exists in a movie. Here I was, 15 years old, staring down the man who had made my life a living hell for three years. He abused me mentally and physically and the wounds were deeper than I may ever know. I stared at that hand for what seemed like forever. Then I looked him dead in the eye and with every ounce of courage and strength I had inside me and said, "I have no father."

I may not know much, but I sure as hell know how to make an exit.

Such a drama queen.

In casual conversation I usually cite this as the last time I ever spoke to him but this isn't the truth. Since that moment we have talked on the phone a handful of times but usually only when it was completely necessary. In truth, the last real time I ever spoke to him was in the fall of 2010. I was making an effort to re-connect with his side of the family all while trying to avoid him. I failed miserably.

It was Thanksgiving and I decided to call my uncle forgetting that my dad would be there for the holiday.

Thinking that I had called to talk to him, my uncle put my father on the phone.

The conversation was quick and painful. He spouted off the same lies I had been hearing for years. He said he missed us kids and thought of us all time. He said he wanted to keep in touch and I should call him again soon. Every word from his mouth felt like acid on my brain.

When I got off the phone I sat down and cried. I felt miserable and regretted ever trying to keep in contact with my family.

That Christmas I did send him a card.

I never got one back.

bohemian rhapsody

I received an email through my blog not too long ago asking if I had a coming out story. While this may seems like a fairly straightforward question, it's actually one that left me a little bit stumped as I pondered the answer.

You're probably thinking to yourself, "Yes. Josh, the answer is yes. You have a coming out story and we all know this. We've seen your blog and you are quite gay."

Thanks?

The fact of the matter is that when it comes to coming out, it isn't just a one and done experience. Unless you're a big celebrity announcing it on the cover of people magazine (I'm looking at you Dumbledore) there's a good chance that you'll find yourself coming out over and over again. As you meet new friends,

That was about the extent of our relationship. Granted, I feel that this is how any middle school relationship should be. Go to the movies, make mix tapes, hold hands. Save the rest for marriage. We never even kissed. She asked me if I was ever going to kiss her. I forget how I answered, but I do know that I managed to talk myself out of the situation.

When we broke up it wasn't the end of the world. Granted, if I remember correctly, she did slap me and then stormed away to the girls bathroom. I think it was less out of anger and more what she thought she was supposed to do when someone broke up with her. I give her points for the dramatic approach to the entire situation. We remained friends up until I moved back to Massachusetts and recently reconnected on Facebook where I learned she is now married to a wonderful woman.

Oh universe, you slay me.

It was also during this time that personal computers and the internet were more common in homes and I was allowed to have my own computer in my room. At the time, this meant adding a second phone line to the house so as not to tie up the main house phone.

Go ahead and add ten points to my coolness jar. I'll wait.

It was with this new connection to the outside world that I could explore the feelings I was having inside. Again, you have to remember the internet back in 1999 wasn't what it is today. At the time there were only about 3 million web sites (compared to 2017's 1 billion plus) and Google was still a baby.

So my explorations were still quite limited but the ability to connect with people outside of the small bubble of Cayucos was amazing. Through sites like LiveJournal and various chat rooms, I met new and interesting people from all over the world.

While it was so wonderful to be able to discover an entire world outside of my small town, I still felt trapped and scared. While I was able to talk through my feelings with random strangers on the internet, I was lacking any sort of role model or even just a real person to talk to.

The only gay characters you ever saw on TV or in the movies were the stereotypical sidekicks. Something I really couldn't see myself identifying with. Gay men were props, someone who existed in the background to be snarky .

In 1997 Ellen DeGeneres made television history when her character came out of the closet as a lesbian. This coinciding with Ellen, herself, coming out to the world on Oprah. You can pretty much pinpoint this moment as ushering in a new era of a mainstream understanding of all things gay. But this coming out wasn't without it's backlash and Ellen's show was quickly canceled.

This act of coming out was so controversial it had cost someone their career. Nearly twenty years later it is a bit funny to look back and remember how people had reacted as Ellen is now a household name. She's basically the new Oprah. We have come so far as a society when it comes to the acceptance of gay people, it is something to be a bit proud of.

But in 1998, in Cayucos, California. We weren't there yet. I was still left without any real outlet for how I was feeling. The show Will & Grace was in its infancy but there was still nothing I could see of myself in the show. The characters were already out of the closet and comfortable with who they were. I was still on the journey where they had already reached their destination.

When it came to the mainstream media the only story anyone was talking about in the fall of 1998 was the brutal murder of Matthew Shepard in Wyoming. While his death did bring about major changes in hate crime laws, it made for a terrifying time to be a young gay man.

It looked like I was on my own.

Freshman year of high school was nothing short of hell on earth. Being such a small town, Cayucos didn't have a high school so we had to be bused to the nearby town of Cambria to attend Coast Union High School.

It was complete shell shock and I found myself in a state of constant emotional overload. Doesn't help that many of my middle school chums and I were finding ourselves in hormonal overload as well. My feelings towards other guys were becoming stronger and as a result I felt like more and more of an outcast. I found myself in a whole new world where there were bigger, stronger and meaner people throwing around insults and homophobic slurs.

I did my best to fly under the radar and kept to myself. For the most part it worked but you'd be amazed at how much attention you end up with when you don't want any at all. I did have a small group of wonderful friends who I loved but I still didn't have anyone I felt comfortable talking to about my feelings.

Worse than that was how much people enjoyed pointing out how different I was. The teasing and tormenting was relentless and I retreated further and further into myself. All the guilt, shame and self-loathing were starting to take their toll on me. These feelings began to manifest themselves into even darker thoughts. Each day I found myself closer and closer to succumbing to these feelings and putting an end to everything.

One afternoon when I got home from school, I found myself home alone. It had been a typical nightmare of a day and for the first time it all felt like too much. All of the pain and frustration I had been feeling all for so long had reached their boiling point and I broke.

My dad kept a loaded handgun in the top drawer of his dresser. I knew it was there and I knew it was loaded. I don't honestly know if he thought I was clueless to its existence or just didn't care enough to keep the thing locked up with the other guns.

I made the short walk down the hallway and retrieved the weapon from its place in the drawer. Back in my room I sat on my bed, feeling the weight of it in my hands. It was heavier than I had expected. Not overwhelmingly so but the thing had a pretty good heft to it.

I sat with that gun in my hands for what seemed like hours, days. I analyzed every inch of it, studying it. I like to know how things work so I sat, trying to figure it all out. It was going to be the weapon of my demise so it was only fair that I understood everything there was to know about it.

Then became the question of how to do it. I mean, I knew the basics, pull the trigger. End of story. But where to aim? The head seemed like a logical choice so I started there. Like I said, the thing was heavier than I expected so holding it at an angle to put a bullet through my temple was proving tricky.

I'm sorry, I really should have warned you that this was going to get dark. Too late now I guess, we're just going to have to tough this out together.

The next logical move was to put the gun in my mouth. Let me tell you right now, guns taste disgusting. I can still taste the oily steal in my mouth even now, over 15 years later, the tang of the metal as it rested on my tongue.

I sat there, silent, hand on the trigger, gun barrel in my mouth and I pulled the trigger.

Nothing.

My dad may not have locked the gun away safely or put a trigger guard on it, but he did store it with the safety engaged.

That safety saved my life.

With the adrenaline of the moment fading I bolted back down the hallway with the gun and put it back in the drawer, the barrel still wet with my spit.

I thought I would never stop shaking.

What the hell was I thinking? Is this really what I wanted to do? No. I didn't want to die. The problem was that I didn't have a clue what else to do either.

In the summer of 2000 I was offered a reprieve and made the move from small town Cayucos to the slightly less small town of Boxford, Massachusetts. I wanted this to be my fresh start, a new chance to become a brand new version of the same lie I had been telling for years.

The possibilities were endless.

My sophomore year of high school saw me as the new kid at Masconomet Regional. I tried my best to go unnoticed by everyone but when people hear you moved to "small-town-nowhere" from California they are going to be interested. I was like the Loch-Ness Monster. People were horrified, yet a bit curious all at the same time. Until they talked to me, realized I was a complete weirdo and proceeded to leave me alone.

I've never really had a problem making friends. I am painfully introverted all while being an insane extrovert at the same time. That sounds like it shouldn't be a thing but it totally is so just roll with it. Within a short time I had managed a tight-knit group of friends and settled into my new life in Boxford.

In that same time I became a serial dater, doing everything I could to maintain the illusion of a straight man. Something I failed at often and miserably. I once dated a girl for eight hours while at the Topsfield Fair with friends. We made out like the disgusting teenagers that we were for the better part of our short time together. I broke up with her on the van ride home.

Is that really even considered dating? Probably not. More like a Karadashian relationship. I'm counting it though. Add another 10 points to the coolness jar. Then take them away because I pretty much sucked at life.

I quickly moved on to another girl who had been with us that day at the fair. I'm fairly certain I did it simply to piss off that first girl but who knows. All that mattered to me is that people saw me with a girl, preferably locked in a disgusting kiss.

I broke up with her two weeks later. This was my new pattern and it continued like that through most of that fall semester.

In January a new student, Kris, came to Masconomet and found himself at the mercy of my weird little group of friends. He was given a haphazardly created schedule as a mid-year transfer and found himself in our photography class.

On the surface Kris was quite unremarkable albeit a bit dreamy. He was Russian-born but American raised. He had strong, thick features without being over the top and curly red hair. As I am a complete sucker for a red-head, I had no complaints about him joining our group. Kris was also a lot like a magical unicorn, for he was something new and different and completely unheard of within the tri-town community.

Kris was bisexual.

Meeting him and the revelation of his sexual identity brought up all of those feelings and urges that I had worked so hard to repress. They were back and stronger than ever. The difference was that I now had someone to talk to. Someone who could help me make sense of what I was feeling. Well, as much as another teenager could.

In the silent privacy of the school's darkroom, I revealed to Kris something I had never shared with anyone. Saying those words aloud for the first time, a giant weight was lifted off my shoulders. For the first time in a long time, I felt like I could breathe again. Kris pulled me into a tight hug and gave me a kiss on the cheek.

I guess if you break it all down, that right there is my coming out story. Well, it's my first coming out story. The first time in my life that I was willing to say it out loud.

I'm gay.

Now, if you are rooting for Kris and I to fall madly in love and ride off into the sunset together, prepare to be horribly disappointed. I was. Kris was seeing a girl from another school and the two were madly in love, apparently.

Midway through that semester, Kris disappeared as abruptly as he had arrived. He had been around long enough to help me feel comfortable enough in my own skin to come out and that was about it. To this day none of us know where he went. We don't even have any pictures of him.

He truly was a magical unicorn. I can only theorize that, with his duty done, he had moved on to another school to help another closeted young boy find his inner glitter bomb. Maybe he went on to become Lady Gaga. We'll never know.

Kris did, however, introduce me to Dylan, the only other gay guy at the school. Until we were introduced I had no idea that he even existed. After slowly coming out to my circle of friends we all banded together to attend a meeting of the school's Gay-Straight Alliance. Until Kris I also had no idea that this had existed either.

I swear to god the boy was a fairy godmother.

As the only two gay guys in the group. Hell, as the only two gay guys in the entire school, Dylan and I were attracted to each other more out of convenience then any real connection. Our first date consisted of the two of us going to his house and making out on his bed for a couple hours.

High school.

Following that first date, that first kiss, there was no denying the truth anymore. I had taken those first steps into a whole new world and survived. I had come out to my friends who had my back and showed me nothing but amazing love and support. I had kissed a boy and very much liked it. It was time to let it all out.

So I did and I haven't stopped since.

Like I said, when you get your membership card into the LGBTQ+ community you aren't done there. First there are the recruitment quotas you need to fill in order to maintain a good standing in the club. Then there's the almost daily coming out story. It doesn't end with that first time, it's something that carries on for the rest of your life.

It took me years to become comfortable in outing myself to others. Even through college I kept tight-lipped about my sexuality. I maintained that it wasn't anyone's business but my own and shouldn't be an important factor in my day-to-day relationships. I still maintain that idea but in a far less hostile way.

As I got older and more comfortable, along with finding myself in a more accepting world, I let my flag fly freely. I found my own subtle ways to let it out without having to turn it into a grand, dramatic performance every time I needed to let someone know I was into guys.

There is no rulebook on how it's done and no one good way to do it. I do know that coming out saved my life. In the short term, it didn't make everything better but it was one less piece of baggage to carry around in life.

loser like me

I would like to say that life after coming out of the closet was nothing but rainbows, sunshine and happy days but that would be a lie. But to say it was an absolute nightmare does feel a little dramatic so I'll just say that it was somewhere in between all of that.

A purgatory of existence.

I recently had a conversation with a co-worker about what it was like for me in high school, especially after coming out. It was early 2001 and a time when a lot of the rights and protections we have today didn't exist. Describing this time period is a lot like explaining to a teenager today what life was like before the internet and cell phones. A dark and terrifying time known as the early 90's.

There were dragons.

They are lucky enough to grow up in this world of seemingly endless information and social media. Granted, it's still not perfect but it sure is a lot better.

When I first came out, I kept the circle of confidence tight, really only telling family and friends. Naturally, the entire school knew at lightning speed. This was before texting was a big thing so this was all done word of mouth. We might have been living in the technological dark ages but we were damn efficient at spreading information, especially when it was something private.

Whether I liked it or not, the cat was out of the bag and the whole world knew. By whole world I mean the entire school, which is your world when you're young. Which is sad to think about. You'd think this would be a huge relief but the reality was, it was frightening in a way I don't know how to describe because suddenly everything was changing and I had no way of controlling it. The term bullying wasn't quite the buzzword that it is today but if I were to put a label on the behavior of my classmates towards me, bullying would be it.

For the most part, I was able to brush off the rumors and snide remarks that were thrown my way. I made the very conscious decision that I wasn't going to let it bother me because, at the end of the day, the problem was with them, not with me. I was a strong, confident and powerful person and I wasn't going to let anyone take that away from me. Which is a crock of shit, but I sure as hell wanted to believe it was true.

The hope was really that they would eventually grow tired of their efforts to make me miserable and move on to something else. Playing in traffic was one idea I had for them but it never really took. Also drinking anything and everything under the kitchen sink. Skydiving without a parachute.

Possibilities were endless.

Before I continue, I very much feel the need to point out that I had a wonderful support system in the form of many of my teachers. Our GSA (Gay-Straight Alliance) advisor was a powerful advocate for the safety of all of her students, especially those in the LGBT community (we had less letters back then). Many of my teachers were supportive and always on the lookout for problems. But they couldn't be everywhere. Some of the worst harassment I received came outside of school hours when I was at work.

Throughout all of high school and college I worked at a small grocery store one town over from Boxford in Georgetown. I had started there shortly after moving back to Massachusetts as a bag boy. Nothing glamorous but we didn't play the allowance game in my house. You wanted something, you worked for it and this was the job that helped finance part of my college career. Not as a bag boy, obviously. By time I left I was working as a manager.

As job offerings in the area were slim, many of my co-workers were also classmates so word of my sexuality was soon all over the store. While many of my older colleagues could have cared less, the younger crowd was less open to the idea of letting it go.

Once cashier in particular, Gary, seemed intent on making my life miserable. Gary was a junior at Masconomet and the one who made sure that everyone at work knew that I was gay. I wish I could say that the way he went about harassing me was at least creative, but looking back it was just typical bullying behavior.

If we were on break together he would mess with my food, one time grabbing it off my plate, licking it at returning it to me. If I was bagging groceries at his register he would make a point to tell me not to get too excited whenever something particularly phallic would come my way like hot dogs or cucumbers. Seriously juvenile crap and my adult self is honestly sitting here wondering how this every really got to me.

But it did.

I eventually reported Gary to management and it was dealt with in the form of a stern talking to and a "shake hands and make up" attitude. Being a teenager I didn't know any better so I accepted this as how the situation should have been handled. In retrospect, it most certainly was not, but it was a sign of the times.

That wasn't the end though, oh no, that would be too easy and as we know by now, the universe isn't going to let me get off that easy. For some time I still received harassment from co-workers and even customers.

There was one group of kids from Georgetown who also found great joy in trying to get underneath my skin. They would come into the store and cause problems and harassed me outside of work in the form of slurs and vandalizing my car. I would receive obscene and threatening phone calls and for a short period after I had become a manager, we would have to have the police come and sit in the parking lot at closing to ensure I was able to get safely to my car.

It was embarrassing and caused me a lot of stress and anxiety.

I would like to say that was the worst of it but again, universe. School life wasn't much better despite having a stronger support and semblance of safety in the form of watchful teachers.

At one point during my senior year my locker was vandalized and set on fire. Not a blazing, evacuate the school fire, but someone had lit a paper that had been sticking out of the bottom of the locker on fire and it left a very noticeable mark. I ended up getting called into the assistant principal's office about it and was promptly blamed for the vandalism.

Teachers were supportive and protective. The administrators, not so much. This was never more evident than when a group of football players attacked me in the hallway. I had stayed a little late in one of my classes to talk about a paper with my teacher and as a result, found myself making the trek to lunch through empty halls. I didn't think anything of it until I rounded a corner to find a group of football players hanging out in the long hallway leading to the cafeterias.

They had spotted me and it was game on.

Their movements were swift and, had this been any other circumstance, their coordination would have been damned impressive. Before I knew it I was surrounded, my backpack and lunch ripped out of my hands. The ringleader slammed me against a bank of lockers and the wind was knocked out of me. I sank to the floor, gasping for air, fairly certain I would never be able to breathe again.

He grabbed me by my jacket, pulled me back to my feet, and shoved me back against the lockers, further winding me. He held my head in place and put his face startlingly close to mine. Despite my best efforts, I couldn't move my face away from his, any energy I had was going towards trying to catch any sort of breath.

"Look at this fucking queer," he snarled. "Faggot wants to make out with me."

For the record, I did not.

"You want to make out with me you fucking faggot?"

"No." I managed.

"You want my dick don't you, you pathetic queer."

That was a hard pass from me.

"Well you're not getting it faggot!" he proclaimed.

It was then that his lackeys let me free and he punched me hard in the stomach. As I sat, curled in the fetal position, gasping for air, he leaned in close and spat, "Why don't you do the world a favor and kill yourself."

They left me in a ball on the floor and lumbered away.

I composed myself and gathered my scattered belongings. My lunch was nowhere to be found and I looked like I had just walked through a hurricane. Beaten and ashamed I continued the walk to the cafeteria. I ended up buying something from the vending machines just outside, not wanting anyone to see me. I slipped into a bathroom and ate sitting in a bathroom stall.

It took longer than I'm willing to admit but I did report the attack, providing names and specific details to my grade's assistant principal. He brought the football coach into the conversation and the two decided on an appropriate course of action. That action being a week of lunch detentions (so not to interfere with football practices) and some extra community service time tacked on to our mandatory yearly requirement of ten hours.

That was all.

Vindication didn't come for another few years when I was approached by one of my attackers at our five-year reunion. He made a point to seek me out and apologized for how he treated me throughout high school and while he didn't specifically mention the attack, it hung there between the two of us like a bad smell.

I wasn't the only new kid the year I began at Masconomet. He had been as well and was just trying to fit in as part of his own efforts to stand out. At the time of our reunion I had just started working as a Bullying Prevention Specialist so I understood his follower mentality, I just didn't agree with it.

In the long-run, I accepted his apology. Truth be told, until I had seen him that night, I hadn't given much thought to him or really anyone else I had gone to high school with. I had grown up and moved on. There was, however, a tiny amount of satisfaction knowing that, while I had moved on, he had been living with that guilt for all those years.

When it really came down to it, my classmates weren't my biggest concern. I could escape them. Even when it came to harassment at work. I could escape. It all happened in a confined period of time and then I left, I was able to walk away from the situation to a safe place.

Cue the dramatic turn of events music.

No place was safe.

The biggest bully during my high school years came in the form of my step-father, Henry. After coming out to my mom, she took it on herself to talk to him about it. Where she was accepting of this revelation he was the exact opposite.

My coming out came just a few weeks after their wedding, which had been something of a shotgun affair. No pregnancy, just a quick turn-around time. He was madly in love with my mom and had been since the two of them were kids. His own true shotgun wedding prevented them from getting together and when the opportunity presented itself all these years later, he took it.

Problem was, he wanted just her, and didn't seem to keen on taking on four kids along with it. But that was the only option and he took it. In an effort to win her love he played the part of a perfect father figure.

I still remember the day he sat me down after he had proposed to my mom. I was still living in California at the time and was visiting for a couple weeks during the summer. It was actually Henry that convinced me to move back to Massachusetts because he loved my mom and wanted her happy and that meant having the family all together.

The grass is always greener on the other side.

I had managed to throw a monkey wrench into things when I came out of the closet. From that moment forward, I could do no right in Henry's eyes and he found every reason in the world to be mad at me. One of my favorite mountain out of a molehill moments came when he lost his head because the bathroom mirror was dirty. Apparently he was under the impression that while I was brushing my teeth, I was spitting on the mirror. Just me. Five other people living in that house but I was the one dirtying up the bathroom.

What he didn't expect was for me to fight back. The bathroom screaming match resulted in me getting smacked and him storming off. As the abuse from him intensified, his favorite mantra became, "go ahead and report me to child services, see what happens to you then!"

That's what got me. I had been in this position before and it hadn't ended well. I knew what happened when child services got involved so I kept my mouth shut. I endured, picking my battles and doing whatever I could to just not be in that situation. I took extra shifts at the store constantly because, frankly, it was a lesser of two evils situation.

The true nature of his hatred towards me came during my senior year in high school. A friend from work had set me up with a guy she knew and he and I went out on a few dates. During one of these dates, the weather turned nasty and caused a delay in me getting home at my designated curfew. Again, this was before we all had cell phones so calling to say I would be late wasn't really an easy option.

I arrived home to find everyone already seated for dinner. Before I could take my spot at the table, Henry ordered me to my room without supper. If I couldn't be home when I was supposed to, then I wasn't going to eat. I protested but ultimately went to my basement room without eating.

Shortly after lying down on my bed I heard heavy steps coming down the stairs and I knew it was him. I sat up in bed as he entered my room in a rage. Before I could say a word he smacked me across the face.

A screaming match broke out and he hit me a few times during this altercation and ultimately ended up with him pinning me to my bed with his hands wrapped around my throat, choking me.

This part I remember vividly.

He looked me dead in the eyes and said, "I want you to remember this moment for the rest of your life. The only reason you're breathing is because I'm letting you."

He released me and stepped away from the bed.

"I love your mother and that's the only reason I'll tolerate a faggot in my house. You want to keep fucking around, that's fine. Just know if you get AIDS we won't be taking care of you."

A few more steps towards the door.

"And don't bother whining to anyone about this, they'll take my word over a queer's."

This wasn't the first and certainly wasn't the last big altercation between Henry and myself but it was certainly one of the worst. I covered the bruises on my neck as best I could and my friends knew better than to ask about them. I did what I was told and I kept my mouth shut.

Unlike my attackers in high school, I never got an apology from Henry and frankly, I don't really expect one. Each battle in life is different and it's how we walk away from each is what will define us down the line.

Throughout my life and career I have faced many forms of bullying and faced them down every time. The truth of the matter is that there is always going to be haters, doubters, and people telling me that I'm not good enough. That I'm worthless. They will always exist. But then there's going to be me, every single time, proving them wrong.

Prove them wrong.

bad luck and hard love

Let me paint a picture for you.

It's Saturday night and you're hanging out at home after a long day of probably doing nothing. You've opted for the night at home because the alternative was leaving the house and having to deal with people and that really doesn't sound like much fun at all. You've made up your mind to fly solo for the twentieth Saturday night in a row, alone, with the cats, holding a marathon of some show on Netflix with a large pizza all to yourself and a bottle of wine.

Life is good.

Then you check Facebook.

At first, it's the usual nonsense: a random inspirational photo that your mom posted that, for some reason, is highly distorted and pixelated, someone complaining about their [fill in the blank], something political and lastly EVERYONE IS GETTING ENGAGED EXCEPT FOR YOU!

If you are anything like me, there is really only one thing to do in this situation: open that second bottle of wine.

Then on Sunday morning when you've woken up from your pizza shame feast and shake off the wine headache, you will join some sort of dating website or app. You will fill out your profile with something you believe to be charming and fun, upload the best pictures you have of yourself, browse around and send some messages. By the following Saturday you have received no messages from anyone that you wanted to hear from and received plenty of messages from creeps and perverts. You delete the app, open a bottle of wine, order a pizza and pass out watching Netflix.

Rinse and repeat.

I have never been very savvy when it comes to the world of dating and love and I find I tend to take a very Liz Lemon approach to the whole thing, "I just wish I could start a relationship about twelve years in, when you really don't have to try anymore, and you can just sit around together and goof on TV shows, and then go to bed without anybody trying any funny business."

Now don't get me wrong, there is nothing more amazing than that electricity you feel when holding someone's hand for the very first time. That amazing awkwardness of going in for that first kiss, praying you read the situation correctly. Staying up late and talking about everything and nothing all at the same time.

These are things that I love.

Then I just want to skip to the part where we're feeling no shame while digging out a wedgie in front of one another and staying in bed all day while trading sexual favors for trips to the kitchen for snacks.

This is the dream.

This is also pretty much my ulterior motive for writing this book. I'm just going to hand it off on each first date I go on and tell you to read it. If you can make it through all this deep dark nonsense and want to come back for a second date, there's a good chance I'm just going to propose right then and there.

The truth of it all is that dating the world of apps and whatnot has become nothing short of a nightmare. I've pretty much tried every dating web site and app the internet has to offer and I can honestly say that I'm not a fan of any of them. I also suffer from social anxiety and have a job that has me travelling more than I am home so the internet seems like my best option a lot of the time.

Well either online or by referral.

Like getting a job.

I have tried the whole "meeting someone in the real world" thing but that has also posed its own problems, because, as a gay man, it's not as simple as approaching a cute guy and asking him out. There is so much more than that.

I explained this recently to my friend Taylor so I'll offer you the same insight I gave her.

Say Taylor and I are hanging out at a bar together, having drinks, talking shit about people we hate and other fun things. As we are enjoying the night we happen to spot and attractive gentleman across the room. We both have the same thought: we'd love to go talk to him, make out with him, maybe even touch the butt.

Statistically, if Taylor were to be the one to walk over and say hello she has about a 75% chance of succeeding in flirting and scoring the digits (seriously, she is a rock star, she is getting those digits.) I, on the other hand, have a 75% chance of one of the following things happening:

A) Making a complete ass out of myself because he's straight, or

B) Getting called a foul name because he's straight and also a bit of a dick, or

C) Getting punched.

For the record, I have had all three of these things happen to me while flirting with the wrong person in a bar. Thankfully not all at once.

"But Josh, why not just go to a gay bar and charm the boys with your smolder?"

First off, despite her best attempts to teach me, Rapunzel has yet to help me perfect a smolder that doesn't look like I just farted and I'm now praying no one noticed. I did try to take a master class with Flynn Rider himself but I kept getting lost in his smolder and the whole lesson was rendered moot.

Second, I'm not really the biggest fan of bars, much less gay ones.

I truly despise the environment of bars because I am officially an old fart. Drinks are expensive, it's loud and you are constantly having to yell, and people tend to be at their stupidest when in those situations. Gay bars are just as bad but so much louder because that is where bachelorette parties go for some reason.

So, through all that I decide that online dating is my best option.

But I'm terrible at it.

So very terrible.

My biggest problem is that I never know what to say in that first e-mail. It's so damn uncomfortable so I tend to aim for funny and charming. This usually results in me coming across as a babbling idiot. Granted, that idiocy has won me a few dates but those don't usually end well. One did result in a relationship but he turned out to be a complete psychopath.

That's a story for another book.

Now, you're probably thinking to yourself, "but Josh, I've read this far in your book and you are so damn charming I would date you in a heartbeat!"

Thanks, but you've never received a message from me on a dating web site.

How about an example!

Here is an actual e-mail I sent to one guy on a dating site shortly after I had moved to Florida and, rightfully, did not get a response. My prompt for the subject matter stemmed from something I read in this guy's profile. Under the section "Most Private Thing I'm Willing to Admit" he had written, "I hate most elderly people I meet. It's bad, but I'm working on it."

Here is the message I sent him:

Good morning,

I must say that there is nothing wrong with disliking the elderly. I have found, over time, that I can't stand about 90% of them. There are some cool ones out there, but now that I have moved here and live among them- I'm starting to hate them.

I was actually driving down from Georgia the other day and had an old man and his wife riding my ass on the highway. I was already going well over the speed limit but that wasn't enough. Rather than move out of his way (as he was obviously in a hurry), I slowed down and sped up accordingly as he either rode my ass or tried to get around me- because I'm a jerk. Eventually he won and passed me but not before he AND his wife flipped me off.

Now that I've relived this story I'm not sure if I hate them or admire their tenacity. I think it's a little of both.

I'm glad to have gotten that off my chest. If you need any more rambling stories please feel free to reply back and I can perhaps entertain you with more delightful stories over a Starbucks latte or other adult beverage.

Best,
Josh

P.S. This message is totally not what I had intended but I feel it fits so I'm sticking with it. God speed.

I should point out that was completely sober when I sent this message.

I say casually but in reality I likely handed him the piece of paper which likely looked like a ball of trash and then bolted from the restaurant before he could react or even read what I had put on the paper.

I don't remember much from the courtship but I know the two of us were quite smitten from the start. Our first kiss happened outside of a Denny's at 4:30 in the morning. I have no idea why we were out at Denny's so late and the concept now seems exhausting but we were young and stupid so, why not?

We did spend a lot of time talking, which to me is the absolute best. We'd spend hours on the phone talking about everything until all hours. That's likely how we ended up at Denny's at 4:30 in the morning, we were probably up on the phone and decided to hang out. You have to remember that texting at this time was an expensive venture and call minutes were free after 9pm so that's when all the talking took place.

I'm old.

We had started dating around Valentine's Day which, as it turns out, is really awkward. We both wondered if we should be doing anything to mark the occasion but weren't sure because it had been like, a week. I ended up compromising by getting the most inappropriate card I could find because I'm me and that's pretty much how I roll.

It's safe to say that, as of sitting down to write this chapter, Ryder was the greatest guy I ever dated. I mean no offense to anyone I might be dating now but Ryder managed to set the bar. He was the first guy to ever buy me flowers. I didn't think that was ever something I would care about but I can still remember how I felt in that moment. It felt so special.

The two of us would spend hours on the phone, talking about our days and getting to know one another. We spent as much time together as we could be it at school, late night after work and homework were done, and all the hours in between. We got to know one another's friends and were as close as two people could be. At one point, I invited him to my best friend's house for dinner with her family. This is actually a bigger deal than meeting my family so you know it was something special.

It was around the time of that dinner that I had started to get really sick. It was getting worse and worse and I couldn't get a straight answer about what was going on. Sore throat, coughing, no appetite- really sexy stuff. The doctor's best guess was that I was having a reoccurrence of Mono, mostly because only I would get Mono twice.

I'm a winner.

As Ryder had never had Mono we weren't able to be as close as we would have liked. By close I mean we wouldn't make out constantly like only 19-year-olds can do.

It didn't stop him from being unbelievably sweet and kind-hearted. He would do everything he could to take care of me, making sure I was eating, checking in on me at school and beyond, even bringing me some sherbert to ease my sore throat. We would still spend time together, cuddling, talking and keeping each other company.

Time passed and I got better. I am notorious for getting really sick with no clear explanation and then getting better just as fast. This happened a lot when I was younger, usually right when my parents wanted to go away on a vacation without kids.

Winner.

Once I got better we returned to the normal course of our relationship with great enthusiasm and things could not have been better. Right up until they weren't.

I will, right here and now, take full blame for the end of our relationship. The fault is mine and mine alone and it is something I have spent years regretting. Not necessarily something I've dwelled on but writing about it had certainly made me want to do some hard-core Facebook stalking.

I've resisted.

For now.

There is an absolutely wonderful song by P!NK called "Leave Me Alone, I'm Lonely" that pretty much sums up how I am as a person when I'm in a relationship or even in friendships. I love to be with that one person that makes me feel so amazing and special, but at the same time I really need space. I get overwhelmed and stressed out and sometimes I need to hide under my blankets and ignore the world for a while.

Rather than explaining any of that to Ryder, I pushed him away. I ignored him, his instant messages and his phone calls. I avoided any of our mutual friends to avoid any conversations about why I was avoiding him.

I was a jerk.

To his credit, Ryder never gave up on me. I loved him for that.

In return, I crushed him.

He finally sought me out at the one place I couldn't escape from him, at work. He waited outside by my car until I was leaving for the night as asked if we could talk. We got into his car and he started driving. We drove in silence for a long time. No words. The song "Wagon Wheel" by Old Crow Medicine Show was playing. I loved that song. If we had a song, it probably would have been that.

We rode in near silence for almost an hour, just the radio providing the soundtrack for the night. It wasn't until he drove me back to my car that any conversation began. He opened up, expressing what he felt about everything that was going on, namely me avoiding him. A big part of his fears came from the last time we had seen each other. He had introduced me to his family and it was also the first night he and I had spent together. Adult sleepover style. He was worried that the combination of the two events had pushed things too far too fast and that was why I was pulling away.

This couldn't have been any further from the truth. I had loved meeting his family and truly enjoyed the time we spent with them and, though I never told him this, I loved him.

I probably should have said all that.

I didn't. I made up some bullshit excuses and rather than admitting that I just needed some space, I closed the door on the relationship.

I regret this more than I could possibly explain.

We crossed paths a number of years later while I was working at the New England Aquarium. He was chaperoning a field trip and I happened to bump into him while I was walking through the building. We hugged and exchanged your standard pleasantries but that was it. My heart yearned to say all the things I should have said before, but this wasn't the time or the place.

With some encouragement from friends and alcohol I found him online and was set to send him a message when I discovered he was in a relationship. It wasn't the outcome I had hoped for but I was happy for him. He deserved it.

The universe brought us together once again in the winter of 2011. Come to find out he was working as a server at a little bistro down the street from where I was living. My sister and I loved the place and were there often so I was shocked that we had never crossed paths before then.

I had been in Colorado on a work trip when I received the news that my Grandmother had passed away. I finished out the trip and returned home the night before the wake. Upset and alone, I found myself wandering down the street to the bistro in an effort to drink my emotions. Ryder was working and, after an obscene amount of wine, I decided now would be the perfect time to say all those things I had kept to myself all those years before.

I was, rightfully, ignored.

It wouldn't have mattered too much in the long run. He was still in the relationship that I had learned about through social media and the two seemed quite happy.

As I sit here now, reflecting on all of this, I can't help but wonder what life might be like if I had just had the strength to come clean about how I was feeling back then. Would we still be together? Would I have gone with him when he took a job teaching in Japan? Would we be married?

All these what-ifs.

I try my best not to live in the past, but this one crosses my mind now and then and I feel the pain from this loss. I know that had I shared my anxieties with Ryder he would have understood and helped me work through them. I know this in my heart because that is just the type of warm and caring person that he is.

We would have figured it all out together.

Hindsight is 20/20 and I'm an idiot.

AUTHOR'S NOTE: I would be a liar if I told you I didn't go back and look at his Facebook one last time while working on this chapter. While I was working on the final revisions I decided "fuck it" and popped his name into the search bar. His profile is pretty locked up at this point so all I can see is his profile picture. It looks like he's standing on a balcony overlooking the ocean in some far off country. He looks happy. That makes me happy.

everybody talks

For the life of me, I couldn't tell you how Fritz and I met. It's one of those great mysteries that I can't quite put my finger on but somehow the two of us came into each other's lives. I do know that a lot of AOL Instant Messenger and Facebook was involved.

I'm talking super early days of Facebook here, in a time before memes.

They were dark times. Like. Erhmagerd.

I know. I'm old.

I do know that, regardless of how we started talking to one other, we hit it off right away. At the time I was living in one of the freshman residence halls at Salem State University, rooming with a friend who was working as an academic mentor.

Can we please quickly discuss the fact that I just referred to my living situation as a residence hall? If you're wondering, that's a lot of fancy talk for a dorm.

Dormitory.

Dorm.

That nasty litter four-letter word is how you'd refer to it if you happened to make it through your college career without joining the cult that is Residence Life. I totally drank the kool-aid. Even after all these years, while writing the word "dorm" in this chapter, I'm terrified that the Director of Residence Life is going to appear in a cloud of smoke (not unlike a demon) and chastise me.

A dorm is where you sleep. A residence hall is where you live.

Are there support groups for former ResLife people?

There should be.

I'm going to make a bulletin board about this. Please come to my program.

Fritz was a non-traditional freshman meaning that he was new to the school but had taken time off between high school and starting college. We were the same age and living in the freshman halls. He was in our sister hall a short walk away.

Our affair was painfully short but for some reason the whole thing had a lasting effect on me. So much so that almost a decade later I think about it enough to put it in the pages of this book.

After a couple weeks of talking through electronic means, I asked Fritz out on a proper date. Well, my version of a proper date which involved a midnight showing of a low-budget horror movie that was playing as part of a horror film fest at a local theatre.

The movie was terrible but the company was top-notch.

As any college student is want to do, we made a 2am trip to Denny's following the movie. Afterwards we made our way back to the dorms and, not wanting the night to end, sat in my car talking until the sun started to peak up over the horizon.

Truth be told, these are some of my favorite moments, be it in a relationship or with friends. Just spending time with one another talking about nothing and everything, learning about someone through their stories, passions and fears.

Take note young readers: this is how you truly get to know someone. Their true self. You're not going to learn anything but the shiny surface of a person through something like an Instagram post or a Facebook status. Real, heartfelt conversation is the way to go. Put away the phones and talk.

Nothing else compares.

Fritz and I had both come to Massachusetts from California and this created an immediate bond. We laughed as we reminisced and longed for all the things we missed about the west coast (In & Out Burger being on the top of both our lists). He had worked for Disneyland prior to deciding to go to college and somehow found himself on the other side of the country. We were both massive Disney nerds (Stitch is my homeboy and Donald Duck is the greatest of the Fab Five- I will fight you) and we spent a great deal of time on that topic.

At the time I wasn't big on kissing on the first date but tonight I found myself breaking all my rules. I have no words to describe the fireworks in that first kiss, feeling him smile as my lips were pressed against his. I'll remember that moment for the rest of my life. He was just that kind of guy. You remember him.

I was so giddy when we parted ways at around 6am that I wouldn't be surprised if I had skipped all the way back to my room. I was on cloud nine.

It was now Saturday morning and I had to work all weekend so I left for Boxford not too long after I had returned to my room. The two of us spent the day texting back and forth. I don't remember much of what we talked about during the day but I do remember our parting words later that night.

I had just gotten home from my closing shift and was doing laundry when my phone buzzed and it was Fritz.

FRITZ: What are you up to?

ME: Not a whole lot, laundry and cleaning.

FRITZ: How fun.

ME: Oh, a real riot. If my life were a TV show, I'd be the commercials.

FRITZ: Then the commercials would be my favorite part.

If that isn't a kick you in the crotch and vomit up a litter of adorable golden retriever puppies moments then I really don't know what is.

I was smitten.

Was I also, possibly, falling too hard and too fast for someone? Absolutely. Don't you worry, that trend doesn't end with Fritz.

We made plans to see each other again on Sunday night once I had returned to Salem and we both had a chance to catch up on homework.

Then he blew me off.

I didn't think much of it because, realistically, we were busy college students and it was only natural that we had saved any and all work for the last minute on a Sunday night. I was swamped with reading, essays, extracurricular activities and a million other things so I didn't let the canceled date bother me.

But then it kept happening.

The week was in full-swing and while I was confused by the radio silence, I still wasn't thinking too much of it. It did bug me that our conversations had turned cold on his end but the busy student excuse was ever present so I let it go.

I finally got a lock on another date night the following week as soon as I was out of rehearsal for the show I was assistant directing for the theatre department. The night arrived and I texted him before I went into rehearsal to confirm our date and received a noncommittal reply.

I was annoyed.

Following rehearsal I reach out again and asked if he wanted to come to my room to watch a movie. He said he was tired and was heading to bed because had an early class. Rehearsal had run really late so I couldn't be mad about that so I let it go.

I needed to make a late-night run to CVS and texted a friend who lived a floor below me to see if she wanted to join me on my quest. I made my way downstairs from the third floor to her room and my path took me through the second floor lounge area.

Sitting there with some girls from that floor was Fritz in the arms of a theatre tech Freshman, Patrick.

So there was that.

We locked eyes as I made my way through the lounge but I kept walking, saying nothing.

I was devastated.

I spent weeks trying to reach out to Fritz to figure out what was going on with many of my messages going unanswered and others with cryptic replies. When I tried to get answers from mutual friends I was stonewalled.

I was crushed.

Worse was seeing him around with Patrick. As far as I know, they weren't dating but they were together a lot and it seemed like I couldn't seem to escape them. It killed me.

This piled on with an insane semester lead to a breakdown on my end. I'm not going to put the blame on Frtiz but it was certainly the straw that broke the camel's back. I was a stressed out double major, taking a full-time course load, working 30 hours a week, teaching at a middle school, on the board of three student groups, and assistant directing the most intense production of Antigone ever conceived.

Something had to give.

I maintain that there is nothing like a good ugly snot-cry and that's exactly what I did. I took a walk to a nearby play ground in the middle of the night and did just that. I bawled my eyes out. I'm talking snot bubble crying here people.

It took me a long time to get over Fritz. A lot longer than I'm willing to admit. I had opened myself up to someone for the first time in a long time and the result was heartache. Every once and while he pops into my head for whatever reason and I feel that familiar emptiness. I had tried to keep in touch via Facebook and text but my messages went unanswered.

It wasn't until a few years later that I learned the truth of what has happened. I was at a friend's birthday party and Patrick's former roommate happened to be in attendance. He pulled me aside as I was heading home for the night and told me everything.

It didn't help.

It turns out that Patrick had told Fritz that the only reason I was interested in him was because I had a bet going on with another upperclassman to see who could sleep with the most freshmen over the course of the year.

I was mortified.

The truth of the matter is this. That bet did exist but I had absolutely nothing to do with it. The most involvement that I had in that wager was I happened to be in the room when it was made. Two upperclassmen in the theatre department created the bet and had a whole system in place as to how it would play out over the course of the year. I had zero hand in it.

For anyone wondering the total number of freshmen I slept with that year was zero. If I'm being honest the total number of people I slept with that year was zero.

Spoiler alert: you really don't have that much sex in college. At least I didn't.

Doing it wrong.

Since learning the truth of what had transpired, I have considered reaching out to Fritz so many times

I've lost count. I've started and erased so many messages to him, wanting to explain that I had nothing to do with something so disgusting. That's not the type of person I am and I would never use anyone like that.

I will admit that I have often find myself searching for his face every time I'm out visiting Disneyland. I'm not even sure he's still working there but that doesn't stop me from looking. I doubt he even remembers me.

Knowing what I do now, what hurts the most was Fritz's willingness to believe Patrick's lies. That he wouldn't even bother to talk to me about it. That stings and I think it's that part of it that really keeps me from wanting to reach out to him. I also have to remember that we were both pretty young and stupid back then. It has been over ten years and that can change a person. I'm pretty sure I'm just going to keep wondering though.

I never approached Patrick about it even though I continued to see him around during my remaining time at Salem State, even working on shows together. I treated him as a friend but I never trusted him after seeing him around with Fritz. Had I known the truth sooner I probably would have refused to work with him at all.

Who the hell knows what he was thinking doing what he did. Did he have a thing for Fritz? A thing for me? Both are a possibility, the latter being more evident the night he showed up drunk to my room one night and tried very hard to get me to sleep with him.

For the record, I don't play like that. Ever.

He was a freshmen, he was drunk and he was one of my residents, it wasn't going to happen. I happened to be chatting with Patrick's RA on AOL when he showed up in my room and I politely asked him to come remove his drunken resident from my space. I was a nice enough person not to report him for being drunk but my kindness ended there.

Looking back on all of this now, what hurts wasn't Patrick's lies but how Fritz fell for them. It truly bothers me that he took Patrick's word at face value and didn't once talk to me about it. Talk to anyone about it. I would hope that any of my friends would have defended me and let him know that I would never do something like that.

One of the biggest lessons I have learned from this experience and many similar experiences is to let people form their own opinion of others. There are plenty of people in my life that I don't get along with for one reason or another and the reasons are mine and mine alone. They are based on my truths and my experiences and unless someone is in some sort of danger, I have no right to impart my opinions on them.

I will fully admit that I am guilty of this and now that I'm aware of it, I'm working on fixing that. I'm no longer falling for the "you must hate this person because I do" mentality.

There are some obvious exceptions to this. If you're dating my friend and you wrong them, I am bound by friendship law to despise you. Those are rules.

On the other hand, if you don't like someone for your own superficial and petty reasons, that doesn't mean I'm going to immediately fall in line. I'm an adult. Maybe I'll come to the same conclusion as you. Let me get there myself.

Again, I'm guilty. I have disliked people because I was told to and I look back on that behavior with disgust. One person I was told to ignore by one friend is now a good friend and running buddy. The one that warned me against her? No longer in the picture.

I can't help but wonder how many amazing opportunities I missed out on because I took another person's opinion and made them my own without giving it a second thought. I shudder to think of what relationships both personal and professional I have lost out on.

I sit here now and find myself wondering what Fritz and I missed out on because of Patrick. Life is full of so many what-if moments and this is a big one for me. Don't let your life be full of what-ifs. It's been over ten years since all of this happened and here I am, sitting in a Barnes and Noble Café wondering what could have been.

I realize how that sounds. I realize just how much I let things like this weigh me down. I also can feel it lifting off my shoulders. All of it. The more I write about all of this the more I'm all about letting it go.

Let it go.

somebody told me

There are two types of pain that I probably wouldn't even wish upon my worst enemy. The first would have to be that of a migraine. They are seriously the worst in a way that I can't even begin to describe to someone who has never had one before. You can lose hours and even days to a migraine attack.

I have been suffering from migraines since I was about nine years old and, on more than one occasion, have been hospitalized because of them. Because of a messed up vein in my head, I can only take over the counter stuff to treat my attacks because anything else could kill me. Loads of fun.

The second type of pain?

Being cheated on.

The first time I was cheated on I was twenty-two. Young and stupid. We had met on my birthday when my friends took me to a local gay club and I got just drunk enough to think that handing out my number was a good idea.

It paid off.

We hit it off and started dating. Things seemed to be going great and I was happy. We became frequent flyers at that same bar and I became close with the bartenders and staff there. It was through those friendships that I learned of the infidelity.

It hurt like hell. I was a pain I hoped I would never have to feel again and worked very hard to make sure it never happened. I guarded my heart and shied away from any serious romantic entanglements for a number of years until it felt safe to come out of my shell.

Then it happened again.

There's a lot that could be said about my relationship with Angus but I'm going to stay quiet on that front. I'm opting for this path mostly because, even though I've changed his name, he would get way too my pleasure from any sort of attention in the pages of this book. As tempting as it is to drag his name through the mud in a very public way, I was raised better than that and I refuse to stoop to his level.

I allowed myself to fall in love with Angus hard and fast. It was one of those relationships where everything just felt right, all the pieces fit into place perfectly. The more we got to know each other to more I saw how much we had in common, from past experiences to future ambitions. Even friends thought we were perfect for each other. There were long talks of the future, living together and sharing a life.

Everything was so right.

Until it wasn't.

I was chatting with George, a friend of Angus' when the conversation revealed that something was very much amiss. Both of us were worried that Angus had been acting a bit off lately and thought that maybe the stress of him getting a new job and having to leave for a month of training was getting to him.

Then the chat took a turn.

GEORGE: Do you mind if I am blunt and ask something?

ME: Sure

GEORGE: Has Angus ever said what I am to him?

ME: Not really

GEORGE: Has he mentioned me as a boyfriend?

ME: …

ME: He has not

This is about the time that the two of us realized that we were being played and the conversation very much went in that direction.

The following day, a Monday, I happened onto Instagram where I spotted a photo of Angus. At first I thought he had posted it until I read the caption: "My man-crush Monday goes out to my gorgeous boyfriend." There was yet another player in the game and the can of worms was opened.

Our already damaged relationship went into a full-on tailspin. Despite all of the evidence (upward of four other guys) Angus denied any wrongdoing or infidelity. Any time I brought something new to the table he deflected and did a song and dance to manipulate my emotions. I, foolishly, bought into so many of the lies. I was so in love and so much wanted to work things out. It was for this reason that I allowed the overly toxic relationship to continue much longer than I should have.

My friend Leslie was going through a similar experience around the same time and she encouraged me to "put on my Beyonce pants" and kick him to the curb. In the moment I was full of that Lemonade rage and was ready to do just that, but that feeling left as soon as I talked to him again.

All too late I came to my senses. I reached out to a mutual friend of ours who had known Angus longer than I had and asked him to be brutally honest with me. He was.

The end result was my telling Angus to lose my number. I removed him from social media and from my life.

With so many players in the game, it was open season on who to blame for what had happened, but ultimately, the responsibility rest solely on my shoulders.

The reality was that, even before my conversation with George, I knew something wasn't right. Something had always felt off. Rather than trusting my instincts, I continued on with the blind ignorance of Mr. Magoo. I had seen red flags up and waving at almost every turn and I ignored them.

Even after talking to George and the Instragram posts and million other blaringly obvious signs, I didn't want to believe it. I had myself convinced that it was all a silly mistake and that I was the only person Angus wanted to be with. I allowed myself to believe this because that's what he told me. Even during the worst of it all, he still maintained his faithfulness and desire to be happy with me. I was certain this was the truth and I would be the one to change him.

Hell, even Taylor Swift was convinced she could make the bad boys good for, at least, the weekend. The truth is this: sometimes people are just bad. Worse than that, those same people have no concept of the wrong that they are doing or the pain that they have caused.

I ran into Angus months after everything ended. Rather, he made a point of approaching me. I was in Magic Kingdom which, funny enough, is where I had been when I had that initial conversation with George. Almost sitting in the same damn spot.

I was doing some work on my phone while waiting for the parade to start when I felt someone tap my shoulder. I looked up to see Angus who smiled and said hello. My immediate reaction was shock followed very quickly by a whole lot of anger. My face showed pure disgust.

"What's that look for?" he asked, oblivious.

I clenched my teeth while a million responses ran their way through my mind in the blink of an eye. I settled on, "you are easily my least favorite person in the world."

He either didn't hear me or chose to ignore that comment and cheerfully continued on, "How have you been? We haven't talked in months!"

I glared, trying my best to process the sheer ignorance and stupidity of this entire situation.

"Fine," I managed.

We stared at each other for a few moments. Well, he stared at me and I sat there doing my best to hold back rage, tears and a lot of foul language.

He shrugged, "So are you just not going to talk to me?"

A million more responses shot through my mind, all of them far too colorful for the environment that I was in. I settled back on, "again, you are my least favorite person in the world."

When chosen carefully, words can hurt a hell of a lot more than a punch in the face and mine landed hard. There was a glimmer of pain in his eyes and he turned and walked towards a nearby bathroom. I was so upset that I was shaking. I took a moment to compose myself and moved to a new spot on the parade route to avoid a second run-in.

Later, when I told a friend about the incident she asked why I didn't flip the fuck out at him. This was a completely valid question and I found myself wondering the same. It was inevitable that Angus and I would cross paths in the parks given how often we were both there and I often thought about what the moment we met again would be like. In my mind there would have been a lot of flipping the fuck out. Ask anyone and this reaction would have been completely justified and the catharsis would have been uplifting.

At the end of it all, being the bigger person felt so much better.

This was someone who lied to me repeatedly, cheated on me, stole from me and shattered my heart. There's a good chance that he may never grasp just how terrible a person he is. Flipping out, yelling, screaming and creating a scene would have given him all of the power and made me look like a fool. Possibly would have gotten me kicked out of Magic Kingdom.

I wasn't going to give him the satisfaction.

It took a long time to find wisdom in all of this. I was hurt. I was angry. I was destroyed. I learned that it's important to take care of my heart and in return take care with others. Through all of these experiences together I've learned that communication and honesty is key to any relationship. It's better to break someone's heart with honesty than with lies. I've learned to do this for others and have received the same in return. It still hurts but a hell of a lot less.

Cheating is such an obscene violation of trust, I have no idea how to put it all into words. Just know that there is almost nothing more evil than to be with someone who looks at you with such happiness and hope and hurt them in a way that they would never think of hurting you. To hurt them in a way that makes it almost impossible for them to trust anyone again.

We are all deserving of love and sometimes it feels like it's never going to happen for us. Looking around and seeing so many people happy when we are alone makes it feel like we'll never get to know that feeling.

But we will.

It took me over thirty years to realize this and going through something like this shakes your faith in that belief. Maybe I'm still learning this lesson.

Who knows.

Here's what I do know. Don't fall in love for the sake of wanting to be in love. Don't start a relationship because you want to be in a relationship. Be honest with yourself and others. Rushed love isn't lasting love.

We'll all get there.

Promise.

love song

As I sit to write this particular part of the story, it's been about three years since Angus and I broke up. This is probably the part where I'm supposed to tell you that, while I write this chapter, the amazing guy I'm dating is making us dinner while I get some last minute work in before calling it a night. Where I tell you I found the one person that I will spend the rest of my life with and this story, in fact, has a happy ending.

This would be true if this were all a fairy tale.

It's not.

The reality? It's 1 o'clock in the morning on a random weekday night. I've poured myself a homemade cocktail and I'm watching a P!NK concert on blu-ray while I work the insomnia away.

It's been three years since my last relationship and I've found it hard to break back into the world of dating for a number of reasons. A big one is trust issues. I've gone out a few times since the breakup and one guy seemed like he was going to be the one to save me, until he witnessed me have a panic attack and then it was all over.

Another issue is that I really don't seem to understand the world of dating as it is today. Look at my track record! The best and more real relationships I've had came from a simpler time when you met people in the real world and wrote down your number on a piece of scrap paper. Today it's all about online dating and Grindr and I just don't get it.

It's not for lack of trying. I've tried, it just turns out I'm really bad at asking people out. Let me share with you my friend Kevin's favorite story of me trying to go out with someone.

I had learned that a friend of mine was recently single and I very much had a crush on him. We were, realistically, casual acquaintances at best and had chatted on and off in various settings and he was always very sweet whenever we crossed paths.

So why not?

The problem is, any confidence I had was lost after Angus. Sure, I don't have abs and I'm far from perfect, but I'd like to think I'm a pretty decent catch. But I lost something in myself when things with Angus went south and I've yet to regain that.

So rather than simply saying "I would like to ask you out on a date" I pussyfooted around the issue and did it all sorts of wrong.

I've really just lost any sort of idea on how dating is supposed to work or how to even ask someone out on a date. If it were up to me, we'd go back to the roaring 1940's when you were at a sock-hop with your best pal and you'd tap him on the should and point to a gal across the room and say, "you see her? That's the girl I'm going to marry." And you did!

Expect replace sock-hop with whatever the cool kids are doing these days and girl with guy because this is my love story.

Time's were simpler.

And awesome.

Back to the story.

I'm fairly certain that the fear of being rejected and hurt has messed me up hardcore. I'm still trying to figure it all out for myself at the this point. I do know that when it comes to asking people out I'm doing it horribly, horribly wrong.

My go-to line when I want to ask someone out is, "hey, would you like to grab a drink sometime?"

I'm sure any dating expert will tell you how terrible of a line this is. First off, it leaves everything open to interpretation. Anyone can grab a drink. It means nothing. Second, it leaves an escape route. Sometime? That could be anywhere between now and three years from now.

Josh, why are you the worst?

So I asked this guy out in my own miserable way and, without knowing it, he managed to call me out on my own bullshit in the most painfully humiliating way possible.

ME: Hey, would you wanna grab a drink sometime?
HIM: Sure, that'd be fun!
ME: Awesome!
HIM: You mean as friends though, right?

Kill me.

Kill me hard.

I totally deserved that though.

Here's the hard truth though, sometimes endings aren't going to be happy. Sometimes the bad guy wins and true love doesn't reign supreme.

Now, before you start writing your "plenty of fish in the sea" letters, don't you worry about me. I have faith that when the timing is right, everything will fall into place. Worst case: there's always a Sarah McLaughlin cat that needs a home.

I've learned from my dating years that we have to go through some truly hard times in order to learn, grow, and appreciate the good. For so long I found myself chasing after romance because I thought that's what I wanted. It's what the world told me I needed.

By the time my parents were my age, they were married and already had Shannon and me. That's what we were told the norm was. You find someone in your early twenties and the two of you settle down and get married and have kids and work forty hours a week and that's what life is.

But that didn't work out too well. I found myself in relationships that were toxic and abusive. I found myself with people who didn't really care about me but I was in too deep and scared. I was scared that if I didn't find that ideal life I was told I needed then I was going to be left behind.

I was doing it wrong.

But was I?

The last thing I'm sad about right now is being single. As tempting as it is, with a couple cocktails in me, to go running to the internet to help me find Mr.

Right, I'm going to go ahead and resist. I've learned so much from all of these experiences and the most important thing I've learned is that before I can love anyone else, I need to learn to love myself. Corny as it sounds, it's the truth.

Take the time to find these lessons in love. They might not always be obvious and they certainly won't always be fun but they are there to help you learn, to help you grow.

I really think Mary Schmich said it best, "don't be reckless with other people's hearts. Don't put up with people who are reckless with yours."

Be careful with your hearts friends.

sex, drugs, and rock & roll

Before we get going with things, I'm going to have to be honest in that the title of this chapter is a tad misleading. If it helps, I'm just as disappointed as you are. I've lead you to believe that we are about to go down a rabbit hole to some dark part of my past where I spent a summer of my youth chasing my favorite band on tour and got lost in a sea of debauchery and became the poster child for every kind of intervention imaginable.

Sadly, my friends, I have none of that for you. Not that some of that doesn't sound like a blast. Back in high school (and probably today if I'm being honest) I would have gladly followed around Simple Plan like it was my job. Matter of fact, we made sure to see them every chance we could.

Today, however, the idea of a general admission rock show with a giant crowd of people pressing ever closer to me, squishing up against a barricade, passing around a single bottle of water to share with strangers, all seems painfully unappealing to me.

Fun fact: that's how I got mono my freshman year of college.

No. There's no interventions needed here. Well, probably a Starbucks intervention. But when it comes to sex, drugs and rock and roll I'm pretty solid. Now, I don't want you to despair, the title of this chapter isn't a complete lie. Nah, there is truth in advertising! This is totally the chapter where I'm going to talk about doing drugs!

Now, don't go clutching your pearls and race to ban me from every library and bookstore in your village. You can relax. It's really not all that bad. And if you're wondering about the sex, that's coming in the next chapter, because I'm fairly certain I get paid by the chapter.

You're welcome.

I'm not particularly proud of my history with drugs, but I also know that's its painfully vanilla compared to others. There is a very good chance that any adult reading this will come out of this chapter thinking, "Hell, I did worse than that LAST NIGHT!" Even better chance of a teenager thinking the same thing.

I am nothing if not an ardent goody two-shoes. While I did dabble in underage drinking, it really didn't start until I was around twenty and was limited to drinks that were basically fruit flavored water. Gateway booze. I didn't get drunk for the first time until my twenty-first birthday and even that was a pretty tame affair.

In May of 2006 there were heavy rainstorms in the northeast that caused a lot of flooding, especially around my parents house. I was living in Salem at the time but still commuting to Georgetown to work at the grocery store. My car didn't fare well in the storms and died a sad little death, causing me to be stranded in Boxford for my 21st birthday.

I was content to spend the evening studying for finals, joined by a 6-pack of Miller Lite that my manager had bought me as a birthday present. My friend Marie was not keen on letting me waste my birthday so she insisted that we head out to enjoy my special day. As most of my friends were still under 21 and it was a Monday night, there wasn't too much to be done so we ended up at Chili's.

The rule was that I was not allowed to order any of my own drinks, which I will tell you right now, was a terrible idea. I did start off with a margarita because it was something I had always wanted to try. I loved it. Then came a series of drinks picked by my friends including but not limited to an Appletini, White Russian, and a shot called the Four Horseman.

The festivities were done early and I was passed off to another friend, Heather, who was responsible for getting me back to my parents. I managed to convince her to take me to Best Buy instead. I couldn't tell you what I bought that night but I managed to spend money as I am want to do when I've got liquor in me.

I think Heather's favorite part of the story happened while we were in the store. She had left me in the movie section and was checking out some video games. I suddenly got very paranoid and started to worry people were judging me.

"Heather! Heather! Heather!" I yelled.

"What?"

"Do you think people know that I'm drunk? I don't want people to know that I'm drunk. That's so embarrassing!"

"Well, if they didn't know they do now."

"What?"

"You're an idiot."

"We should go, I'm drunk."

She gathered me up and escorted me to the cash register.

"Did you find everything okay?" The chipper cashier asked.

"I've very drunk, please don't judge me."

"Um."

"It's my 21st birthday and I'm drunk."

"Happy birthday?"

"Thanks, I want some movies."

And that was my 21st birthday in a nutshell and the first time I had gotten drunk. The reality was, I really wasn't even that drunk because I had made sure to keep food in my stomach and well hydrated. I didn't even have a hangover the next morning.

My constant fear of getting into trouble coupled with my anxiety kept me on the up and up through high school and even into college.

I had gone to a small handful of parties but I was always the boring, sober one. I once brought a 6-pack of IBC Root Beer to a college party, like an adult. I was once invited away for a weekend of teenage nonsense one summer during high school, but I was really only invited by default. I was the only one of my friends with a car and a license. Otherwise, I probably would have stayed at home building Lego sets. I love building Lego sets.

My friend Allison's cousin had the run of her family's house in New Hampshire for the weekend and invited a bunch of people up. We drove up Friday night after I had gotten out of work and it took forever for us to get there, arriving well after midnight.

This was long before the time of GPS and my Nokia brick phone's most advanced feature was the game Snake and its ability to hold a charge for roughly one million years. All of this was useless in New Hampshire since cellular service up there was virtually nonexistent. Pretty much still is.

We were driving blind and the printed out MapQuest directions weren't the biggest help. Regardless, we made it. Tired and frustrated, but we made it.

Saturday was a day for sleeping in, hanging out by the lake and just generally being stupid teenagers. Apparently the true madness was being saved for when the sun went down.

I can't remember if someone showed up later in the day with alcohol or it had already been there waiting but once the sun went down it began to flow. Funny thing is, I really think it had been there all day but everyone waited because, as teenagers, it was believed that we saved the drinking for after dark.

We were clearly fools that knew nothing of the wonder that is brunch and bottomless mimosas.

Either way, people started drinking and I was having none of it. Everyone, including the friends I had arrived with, were drinking in excess and there I was, stone sober and petrified that at any minute we were all going to be arrested. I assumed that SWAT was lying in wait for the perfect moment to come crashing through the windows and propelling down from helicopters to take us away.

As the evening went on, my inner parent was both enraged and disappointed in everyone. I was a giant ball of pissed-off anxiety at this point and right when I thought it couldn't get any worse, it did.

Allison's younger cousin and his friends decided to go swimming, the beer was running low and someone knew a good weed dealer that was close by. We needed a beer run anyway and the dealer could hook us up with anything we needed.

I was fairly certain that everyone at this party was trying to kill me if not themselves. While I couldn't put a stop to the drunk swimming, I could put a stop to any plans to acquire drugs and more alcohol.

What everyone didn't realize that, while they were drinking and carrying on, I was wandering around the house and collecting everyone's car keys. Over the course of a couple hours, I had managed to get my hands on every set of keys in the house and had locked them in the trunk of my car. The house phone had also ended up in my trunk as well. Once people realized they couldn't find their keys they figured they'd call for weed and beer.

I will admit, watching everyone stumble around trying to remember where their keys were was actually amusing to an extent. Even better was watching people trying to climb trees in an effort to get cell phone service, so desperate to keep the party going.

Having done my best to secure the drunken idiots for the night, I went to bed deciding that anything that happened after that point was on them because I was tired and didn't feel like babysitting anymore.

To this day, I am still very much a parent when it comes to hanging out with my friends and drinking. I will forever be the one telling people to text me when they get home and will stay up and worry when I don't hear from them. I will force people will stay over at my house if I feel they aren't able to get home safely.

That all said, I am a lot like Britney Spears in that I'm not that innocent. I'm guilty of doing some pretty stupid things in my life. While my shenanigans do range more towards the vanilla side of things, I'm still fairly good at getting myself into some pretty moronic situations. A prime example of this would be the first time I smoked pot.

I have smoked pot a grand total of twice in my life. I am quite often mistaken for someone who smokes regularly but this is far from the truth. Two is my magic number. Both times I tried it, it did nothing for me. I have actually found, over the years, that I am quite immune to all the things that people seem to love.

I have been put on painkillers a few times and they have done nothing for me. When I was twenty-four I had developed a painful cyst on my tailbone and was given Vicodin for it. I was warned to wait until I was safely home to take them and once I had, I was to stay put and not do anything that would harm myself or others. I was told to take them and go straight to bed since the side effects would be intense.

Nothing. I felt nothing.

Once I realized that ibuprofen did the same job but was less terrifying, I dumped my prescription and switched over. The same thing happened a few years later when I had my wisdom teeth removed. I was told I would be miserable and in pain and unable to function for days. I was on my feet and attacking life as normal the next day and found myself dumping yet another prescription into the toilet. When I had surgery on my leg, I told the doctor not to bother with hardcore painkillers. Load me up with 800mg of ibuprofen and send me on my merry way.

I pretty much feel the same way when it comes to pot. It does absolutely nothing for me and therefore I don't bother with it.

My first time smoking pot was during a trip to New York City when I was twenty-three. It was my first visit to the Big Apple and I had been invited to attend the taping of the Bravo A-List awards. I invited my friend Emmy along as she had been to New York before and could show me the ropes. We arrived the day before the taping and spent a good chunk of time being absolute tourists before getting ready for the show.

The filming was a lot of fun to watch and it was amazing to see how something as big as an award show came together. The show was being pre-taped so this allowed for flubs and as a result we were privy to moments that didn't make the broadcast or were censored. It was really cool to watch the show a few weeks later on TV and be able to spot moments that were edited, altered or taken out all together.

After filming wrapped, we made our way back to the hostel where we were staying in Harlem. I will be the first to admit that, while the place wasn't anything like the horror movie, it was still not the greatest situation in the world. It would be a few more visits to the same hostel before I learned to just spend the money on a hotel and call it a day.

On our way back we stopped at a bodega and picked up some beer to enjoy on our last night in the city. We joined some of our hostel-mates in the backyard, drinking and swapping tales from various adventures around the city and beyond. I will say that one thing I really enjoyed about the hostel life was the opportunity to meet and talk with people from all over the world. We were surrounded by young travelers looking to explore and have a great time. A great time was had.

We sat in a circle around a makeshift fire pit drinking and talking into the night. At some point someone fired up a joint and began to pass it around. At this point I was caught up in just about everything about the evening and was having fun. We had spent the night rubbing elbows with some of Bravo's biggest stars, were staying in a shitty little hostel, and I had a pretty decent buzz going on. Why stop the party now?

Despite my buzz, I was still pretty observant of my surroundings and noticed that no one in the circle had passed on taking a hit. When the joint found its way into my hands, I didn't want to be the odd man out. I took a deep puff and let the skunk-tasting smoke fill my lungs.

I coughed like the pathetic nark that I am.

I honestly feel like everything that followed was more driven by alcohol than pot mostly because I started drinking as much as possible to get the horrid taste out of my mouth.

Emmy had been flirting with a guy from Spain who happened to be staying in our shared room. Our first night in the hostel we had been lucky enough to have the room meant for eight people to ourselves. For tonight the Spaniard would be joining us. Thankfully he seemed really nice and we got along well.

Too well as it would turn out.

Sometime during our little drum circle, while I was chatting with two girls from Australia, Emmy had disappeared with the Spaniard. This fact was lost on me until one of the Australians pointed it out when I tried to call it a night and head to bed.

"Mate you may want to wait a bit," one of them said, stopping me.

"Nah, we've got to be up early, I gotta call it a night."

"No mate, I mean your friend is getting laid."

I had been sexiled from the room. The only thing left to do was wait it out. As almost an incentive to stay outside more beer had shown up at some point and another joint was being passed around.

When in Rome?

Sometime later, Emmy and the Spaniard emerged from the room and joined the circle. I was past buzzed and in the early stages of drunk. My senses, common and otherwise, were lost in a haze. Emmy sat down on one side of me and the Spaniard on the other, both looking quite pleased with themselves. I tried to be annoyed that I had been locked out of the room and couldn't go to bed, but I was having fun and being social so I let it be.

"So that was fun," Emmy half-whispered to me.

"Well that's nice." I replied, not really sure what she wanted from me.

"Here's the thing though, he said he can keep going."

I was instantly annoyed because I didn't want to get stranded on the couch in the common room for the night. Sensing this, Emmy continued.

"With you."

Almost on cue, the Spaniard began rubbing my thigh as I gave Emmy by best, "what the fuck" look.

"He wants you."

He leaned in and began kissing my neck as his hand travelled further up my leg.

This entire situation has earned itself a spot in the 10 ten stupidest things that's ever happened to me. Not quite number one but it certainly has a strong hold on its position.

The next morning I woke up and was thrilled to be experiencing my first ever hangover. I felt like crap. My mouth had reached a level of dryness that even the most barren deserts would have been a rainforest by comparison. My head felt as if the cast of Stomp was rehearsing in there, with jackhammers.

Both Emmy and I were on the struggle bus that morning and as a result missed our actual bus back to Boston.

My second and last dance with Mary Jane came about a year later. I had moved into a new apartment and we had made friends with the guys renting a place across the street from us. One night that summer we ended up over at their place for drinks. Once again I found myself sitting in a circle of people, drinking and talking and soon enough a joint found its way into my hands.

Not wanting to be rude, I took a puff each time it made its way around to me.

Nothing.

Since that time I have learned to just say no. I've have found myself being offered bongs and joints but I've declined each time. It wasn't for me and never would be. I hold absolutely no judgment towards those who do smoke, I just don't enjoy it myself. I'd rather put my money towards something that does work for me. Like wine. Wine always works on me.

When it comes to pot, I still have friends who I know smoke regularly and that's great for them. I have gone ahead and voted many times for legalization of the stuff, not because I have any interest in it, but because my responsible adult side sees the potential for economical growth from the pot industry.

I'm such a nark.

toxic

"Well that's not what you want," I said to absolutely no one.

It was 1:30 in the morning and I was sitting in my car in the parking lot of the restaurant where I was working as a waiter. I had just finished up my shift, an absolutely horrendous double that had me there from open to close. I was tired, cranky, my feet hurt and I had just gotten a text that no one wants after a day like that. Frankly, a text no one ever wants to get at all, period.

"Sorry for adding to a shitty day," he wrote.

"Could be worse." I replied.

It could have been. Could have been much worse.

Logan and I met while I was on trip to Portland, Oregon to speak at some schools. He worked at the coffee shop that was attached to the hotel where I was staying. There was some hardcore flirting while he took my order and, in an act of bravery that I would never have the guts for, he put his number on my cup.

Side note: this stuff only every happens to me when I'm on the road. I excel at getting numbers from guys who live thousands of miles away. Guys close to home want nothing to do with my nonsense. Guys who are literally out of my reach? I am gold.

I had to applaud the move and I shot him a text after I had left the shop. I was speaking at a local school and had some free time between programs so the two of us grabbed lunch. Our time was limited but there was certainly a spark between us. It was a great feeling and certainly something I hadn't experienced in a long time.

There's a lot to love about life on the road but the downside is having the opportunity to meet amazing people and find connections all over but never getting the chance to see them again.

Single serving friends.

I was afraid this would be the case with Logan but, thankfully, the universe had other plans and for once they didn't involved screwing me over. The two of us stayed in touch through text and social media long after I had returned to Orlando. When I got booked at a school that would have me returning to Portland, I let Logan know and the countdown until we were reunited began.

Now, to be perfectly clear, we both knew that no relationship was going to be growing out of whatever it was we were doing but a friendship was more than enough for me. Having a familiar face when you're thousands of miles from home is the most comforting thing in the world. It also helped that he's not too hard on the eyes either.

When scheduling my trip, I purposely left some chunks of time surrounding my speaking engagements and travel arrangements. This allowed Logan and I time to see each other without worrying about lunch breaks ending or catching flights. Unlike when we met, there was no time crunch.

He had me meet him at his place and we walked around the area for a bit looking for a place to grab lunch. It's always great to have a guide when in an unfamiliar city, especially when it comes to food. I have a rule when I'm travelling that I will only eat at places I can't find back home. This eliminates most chain places.

The exception is In-N-Out Burger. That place is my first stop whenever I'm in California. Frankly, I don't understand how anyone I know in California is as healthy as they are. If I lived that close to In-N-Out that would be my all-day, every day meal.

Now I want animal fries.

Back to Portland.

After lunch we found ourselves directionless so we ended up pointing ourselves back to his place. We shared a kiss while standing in his kitchen. Soon, one thing led to another and we found ourselves in his bedroom. Caught up in every moment as the rating of the situation moved from a PG-13 to an R and beyond, we fell deep into one another.

The sex was amazing. The sex was mind-blowing. The sex was unprotected.

Learning about sex as a gay teenager was a trial by fire kind of experience for me as it was, and still is, for so many gay youth today. Sure, I was put through the banal videos of boys who's voices have changed, girls who have started shaving their legs, and plenty of material about the ins and outs of sex between a man and a woman.

When it came to me. When it came to a man having sex with another man, there were no lessons. The only really meaningful tidbit that came out of all of those lessons was that HIV was bad and we were all going to die.

Sounds over-the-top and dramatic but frankly that's all I really seemed to get out of the few moments dedicated to the topic when I was thirteen.

Honestly, thinking back on all of it now, I feel like we really weren't taught much of anything in those classes. Sure, we were told about condoms and safe sex but we never talked about how to go about having that conversation with a sexual partner. They taught us about getting tested but they never told us what that really means or how to go about getting it done. Sex Ed was one of those classes where you walked out with more questions than answers.

Now would be a great moment to hop onto my soapbox and go on a rant about how schools are failing in preparing students for the real world in a number of different ways. I see it as a major problem that we seem content with never dealing with. More so, when it comes to the sexual health of students, there is a major gap between what is being taught and what really needs to be addressed.

When it came to the sheer mechanics of sex, I don't think anyone really got anything out of our classes. Sure, maybe I would have gotten at least a little bit out of it all if I were attracted to women but in the end I was more clueless then my classmates. As a result, I had to take lessons from the world of the internet and badly pixilated 30-second long RealMedia clips.

I learned about sex from porn.

Fun fact: porn is not real life.

My first experience with sex was fumbling and awkward at best as I assume it is for all of us. This was mostly because we had no idea what we were doing and no one beyond an America Online connection to teach us anything. We knew we needed a condom and had a rough idea on how to put it on. Did you know it's illegal to show student how to use a condom in a live demonstration? Not with an actual penis, that would be absurd, but even with a banana or a cucumber. As least this is what we were told. I don't know what is true anymore.

Learning about sex in the real world came about through trial and error. Mostly error. The learning process was a slow one. We are still talking the early days of the internet though we had taken a step in the direction of cable modems but the ease of access to the kind of information that would have been helpful was still non-existent. This made life frustrating.

As I mentioned before, the gay population in my high school was very much limited to Dylan and myself and we were a relationship of convenience. My first time had been with him and, upon reflection, I regret that fact. We were together because there were no other options. Maybe we thought we had feelings for each other but it was likely just repressed teenage hormones. He was my gateway relationship, my first step into the gay world.

There was a grand illusion that everything would change once I got to college but I was quick to learn this wasn't going to be the case. Sure, I was a smaller fish jumping into a larger pond but in the days before Tinder and Gindr, meeting a guy was difficult at best.

Ryder and my relationship came about during my sophomore year in college and my experiences at that time were limited to a few awkward attempts at sex with Dylan.

There's a lot of talk of experimenting in college to help someone develop their sexual identity. Take that to mean whatever you'd like, be it experimenting with your sexuality or learning those fun little things that you enjoy in the bedroom. Feathers? Leather? Tax returns?

College was the place to learn it all.

Unless you're me.

When Ryder and I broke up, the world of social media was starting to bring people together more and more. Facebook had us connecting with classmates in new ways and it cracked the door on a whole new world.

I am not one for hook-ups. I've never really been able to wrap my head around it, I'm the type of person that desires a deeper connection. That being said, I'd be lying if I said I never had hooked-up with anyone. College was a time to try new things and at that point the world will still pretty damn new to me.

I hated it. I have walked away from those situations feeling nothing but remorse simply because I knew it meant nothing. At the same time, I walked away with the experience and knowledge I was lacking. I discovered that when you are sharing the experience with someone you will likely never see again, you're far less inhibited and are more willing to just go for it.

It was porn.

No, I wasn't doing porn but I was basically doing what I knew. I had received my sexual education from porn so it only made sense that I sought out similar experiences. It wasn't until sitting down and writing this all out that I finally made that connection. Definitely not my proudest "ah-ha" moment of the book but there it is. Oprah would be proud and a little ashamed, mostly ashamed.

The problem is that there are things that porn doesn't show you about the real world of sex with one of the biggest being communication. I can't name a single video that I've seen, be it made in a studio or homemade, where there is sort of conversation regarding consent. Not one. And I've watched a lot. Obviously for research purposes. I'm not a monster.

Second to consent is a conversation about safe sex. There's no discussion of testing, STDs, or condoms. In most porn, the condom just magically appears out of nowhere and everyone is just going about their business as if that's completely normal.

It's not.

When it comes to my sex life, I relish my clean lifestyle. While I may not have always had the "when the last time you were tested/what were the results" conversation, I have always been sure to practice safe sex. After my break-up with Angus, I made getting tested a more regular occurrence then it had been before. We had been in, what I thought was, a committed relationship and we had unprotected sex. If he was willing to do that with me, how willing was we to do that with the other guys he had been sleeping with?

Better safe than sorry.

But if you have learned anything in this book, it's this, I'm human. I make mistakes.

With Logan, I allowed myself to get caught up in the moment of passion happening between us. When you are that connected and everyone is having a good time, no one wants to be the guy that stops it all for a boner-killing conversation like that.

I'm here to tell you right now, have that conversation. It's a lot better than this one:

"Hey you," he texted.

"Hey! I was just thinking about you today, I just found out I have strep throat and I might have been contagious when I saw you."

"Funny enough, I thought I was getting sick and I went to the doctor. I was tested for strep and it came back negative."

"Lucky you, strep sucks." I replied.

"I do need to tell you that I tested positive for Chlamydia though."

I would like to take this moment to point out that spell-check automatically capitalizes the word Chlamydia because apparently it's a proper noun. Let's give Chlamydia the respect it deserves.

"I'm sorry," he followed. "All my other tests came back negative though."

"Could be worse," I said and put my phone down to drive home. My indifference stemmed from being way too tired to start to even begin to stress about this in the moment. It was 1:30 on a Saturday morning and I was two days away from being able to do anything with this information.

Logan was sweet in his constant apologies. He felt terrible for putting me in this situation and I appreciated that. The truth was that we were both adults and we made an adult decision. I couldn't be mad at that and I told him as much.

I was more disappointed in myself for putting myself in this position. If life has taught me anything at this point it's that, rather than dwelling on our mistakes, we need to learn from them and move forward.

So I learned and I moved forward.

The first step was actually finding myself a doctor. My old primary care physician had gone out of business with no warning and I had been without a doctor for a good chunk of time. I used this situation to get my act together and find someone new.

What made this all so much worse was not only was I going to have to have this conversation with my doctor but it was going to be a doctor who was a complete stranger to me.

"Hi, I'm Josh, your new patient. First order of business will be some STD testing because I'm and idiot who's been exposed to Chlamydia with a capital 'c' because spell-check says so."

I make for a grand first impression.

Thankfully, despite being one of the most awkward conversations I've ever had, the whole thing went well and without a lecture. I think she could tell how stupid I felt about the situation and spared me. There's really nothing worse than being thirty-one years old and receiving a talking-to usually reserved for pre-pubescent teenagers. Granted, many adults are as stupid and childish as pre-pubescent teenagers so the lecture wouldn't have been without merit.

Next came actually getting tested. Despite being exposed to just Chlamydia, I asked for the whole enchilada. Go big or go home. Mercifully, the tests were batched in with my routine wellness checks so I felt like less of a man-whore when handing over the orders to the nurse at the testing facility.

Then came the waiting.

The time between that text from Logan and actual-ly sitting down to get blood drawn was about a month. The delay was caused by how long it took to get a new patient appointment with a new doctor followed by getting an appointment for the tests. American health care at its finest right there.

The bonus? Ignorance is bliss, right? You can't fear the answer if you never ask the question. But the ques-tion had been asked and for another three long days I sat and feared the worst for the answer. My anxiety and general, over-active imagination, had the test com-ing back with all sorts of bad news and I all but planned my funeral right then and there.

With what can only be described as sheer, dumb luck, my tests all came back negative and I was still my normal healthy self. Physically healthy that is, I'm still mentally ill like a boss. The news was a relief and I thanked my lucky stars for the positive outcome. I was also very thankful for the all-important lesson that I received through all of this.

Finding myself in this awkward situation gave me time to reflect on some of the decisions that I was mak-ing in regards to my body and my health. The period of time during which I had no idea what my status was became something of a dry spell for me as I didn't want to risk potentially spreading something to anyone else. No one wants to be that guy.

Like I said, I'm not really a "one and done" type of guy and I would certainly prefer a long-term committed relationship over a one night stand. I can't say for sure that the next guy I have sex with will be the guy I spend the rest of my life with, but I'd like to think that may be true. If I'm lucky.

Which I'm not.

Being in this position did give me pause to think about what I really wanted. I hate the feeling that comes over me following a hookup with someone. I've tried that whole "friends with benefits" thing as well and it still didn't feel good. If felt just as bad to share something so special and intimate with someone, but harbor no romantic feelings whatsoever. Not for me. It's a torturous cycle.

I managed to get lucky this time but how long until that kind of luck runs out?

I've now forced myself to have that awkward conversation more since this all went down. I have stopped moments dead in their tracks to say, "if we're doing this, we need a condom." I don't care if you tell me you're squeaky clean and have been blessed by the pope. We play safe or we don't play at all.

Let's all learn a lesson here and take the time to have this awkward conversation, regardless of who you are sleeping with. From one night stands to long term commitments, take the time to be safe and healthy.

details in the fabric

The post said it all, though at the time I didn't know just how much. It was a Friday afternoon and I was sitting in the parking lot at the restaurant where I was working part time. My shift was set to start in about fifteen minutes. It was an Instagram post. The silhouette of a lost soul, clutching his head, lines blurred.

It wasn't a picture of me. I'm not sure who he is or even where I found the picture to begin with. Nevertheless, in that moment he was me and I him. Both clutching our heads, trying to silence the screaming coming from within. An unknown yet familiar and painful voice.

The caption read "Depression is an evil, nasty little bitch and I absolutely refuse to let it win. If I'm being honest, it's got a pretty good lead on me right now."

I don't know when exactly this episode started but I can pinpoint the moment when I was willing to acknowledge it. It was the day before, Thursday, and I knew something wasn't right and I said as much to a friend in a text message Thursday afternoon.

"I think I may be on the verge of a breakdown"

Looking back, I'm fairly certain I knew the truth in that moment but I didn't want to believe it, I didn't want it to be real. I wasn't on the verge, I was there. I could feel it in every ounce of my being but I didn't want it to be true. But it was true. I was on the edge and going over.

Friday morning I woke up and I couldn't function. I managed to get out of bed only to find myself on the couch. I stayed hidden under the safety of my favorite green blanket until I had no other choice but to get up and face the world.

Back to the parking lot. Friday afternoon.

I'm not okay. I know this. I can't let anyone know. I bury it. I sit in the parking lot holding back tears. Fighting off the bad feelings, the bad thoughts, the screaming voices.

Triggered.

Triggered has become a fad phrase. Have you noticed? People like to joke that a meme, a photo, a situation has them triggered. Who the hell knows what they think they mean by this. Maybe they think they are funny.

Maybe they are.

Do you know what it's like to really be triggered?

Here I am, ten minutes from having to clock in for my shift in a busy bar on Saint Patrick's Day. I can barely breath, I want to scream, I want to cry, I want to close my eyes and never open them again. Something has me triggered. Really, truly, triggered.

It's not as cute as you'd think. This isn't a meme or a viral video. This is real life. This is my reality. This is terrifying. My heart is racing to the point where I actually think I might be having a heart attack. I'm sweating and feel like my body has reached a million degrees but feel like I'm going to freeze to death all at the same time. I'm thinking ten thousand thoughts all at once but nothing at all. My hands are shaking as I grip the steering wheel of my car.

I try to find calm. I try to find control. Breathe in. Breathe out. Inhale and exhale. Do all the things you're supposed to. But I can't.

My mouth is dry. My throat feels tight. Even breathing feels like a massive undertaking. I hold tight on the wheel hoping to feel grounded. Feel some stillness and calm while there is a storm raging in my head. I'm afraid. I'm really afraid and this isn't the worst of it. Not even close.

That's still to come.

But I have to go to work. I can't call out when I'm sitting in the parking lot and my shift is about to start. How do I even begin that call? I can't come in because the voices in my head are screaming?

They say that in these moments that you can calm yourself with breathing exercises. I don't know who 'they' are but sometimes they can go fuck themselves.

I hate them.

But I breath. I'm far from calm but I walk into work and no one is the wiser.

I was diagnosed with depression sometime after my parents got divorced. I had gone through a kleptomania phase and was stealing money from my mom and her boyfriend. The answer was therapy.

I remember Shannon making fun of me because I had to visit the shrink. The head shrink. "She's going to shrink your head!" Having no idea what that meant, the whole idea of what was happening terrified me and I remember kicking and screaming the entire way there. My fears were quickly alleviated on that first meeting and I really liked the woman who would be shrinking my head. She had me tell her stories.

I love telling stories.

I was never put on medication following the diagnosis. I'm not sure why. Maybe there were none suitable for kids at the time. Maybe my mom didn't want to go down that path. Maybe I'm wrong and I was being secretly medicated the entire time. Who knows? That sounds like something my mom would have done.

It wasn't until 2013 that I was also diagnosed with post traumatic stress disorder along with a generalized anxiety disorder. It would turn out that I had been suffering from the effects of PTSD for years but they went undiagnosed simply because I didn't know any better. It wasn't until after the events of the Boston Marathon bombings that my attacks were frequent enough to warrant a conversation with my doctor.

Turns out there are many events that I have blocked from my memory and as a result I'm never sure what triggers my attacks. Some things I have begun to recall recently as I've been working on this book. Many of them are here on these pages, but who knows how many are still buried somewhere deep down inside.

So when it comes to March 17th of 2017, I don't know what was triggering my attacks. So I buried the pain, the panic and the depression. I put on my big ole smile and I clock in for my shift.

Working while in a persistent state of panic and anxiety was definitely not the smartest idea in the world. Many times throughout the night I found myself clutching either side of my head, hoping and praying that the screaming inside would stop.

The perk of working in a busy restaurant is that very few people are actually paying attention to you unless you've screwed something up. So whenever I disappeared to the bathroom just to get a few minutes away from it all, no one noticed. I was on top of my rotation, my guests were happy and no one noticed anything was amiss.

The perk of mental illness? It's not a broken leg or stitches. It's not the flu or a deformity. It's hidden away and no one can see it. No one knows anything is wrong. The downside? No one understands because it's not a broken leg or stitches. It's not the flu or a deformity. No one can see it. No one can tell anything is wrong.

When I did lash out through the night it was easily excusable. Have you ever worked in a restaurant? It's all laughing and smiles when you're on the floor but put us in the kitchen and we're at each other's throats. Me yelling at co-workers, like I did a lot of that night, no one gives it a second thought. It's busy, we're all in the weeds, and no one is happy. I'm just less happy. I'm more than less happy. Something ugly is brewing.

At some point in the night my brain simply went into auto-pilot. My vision narrowed and I reached the point where I was just going through the motions of being a human being. I left that night, forgetting to clock out. I never forget to clock out. This is minor in the grand scheme of things but major in my mind.

In the calm and quiet of my home things start to get truly terrifying. A small thought, born in the furthest and deepest part of my mind has slowly started growing, moving to the forefront until it's an a giant semi-truck that I have no time to get out of the way of.

I want pain.

It had been well over a decade since the thought of hurting myself had crossed my mind. So long that I haven't bothered to keep track because, frankly, I thought that part of my life was over. I thought it had gone away forever.

I thought I was better.

Better, not best.

The first time I had cut myself was a distant memory from what seemed like a whole other life. During that time, when I was an angry teenager filled with the angst and anger. It was in that time that I hurt myself because I was mad.

I honestly wish it were something far more poetic than that but the truth of the matter is, I was angry. I was fighting with my step-father, Henry, about god only knows what. We were always fighting. He hated me. I hated him. It was the nature of our relationship. Sometimes it turned violent, other times it was just words.

One day we were fighting and I stormed down to my basement room where, in a fit of rage, I grabbed a box cutter and tore into the flesh of my inner thigh. I had gone into a fugue state and wasn't fully aware of what was going on until the next thing I knew, blood was running down my leg.

The damage was minimal but real. I was dumb-founded by what I had done and worked quickly to patch myself up and pretend it never happened. It wasn't real. It wasn't me. I swore to myself it would never happen again.

Until it did. Again and again.

Eventually, I moved away from this practice and channeled those feelings in other ways. I regressed back to my old comfort of eating my feelings and used food to ease my pain and frustration. Over time I learned to manage it all in healthy ways while sometimes backsliding into destructive behavior. Each time, I learned, I grew and I worked to move away from hurting myself.

This is what made these feelings so scary that night. It was something that had been buried for so long I thought that it was gone for good.

Between depression and anxiety pouring over me, I was in a lot of pain. Physical, mental, everything. It was overwhelming and the screaming in my mind was enough to drive me insane. I wanted control. I wanted to feel control. I wanted to channel and control that pain. I wanted to feel like I could have power over something, anything, everything. If I could just feel it, control it, harness it, maybe I could make it go away.

It's two in the morning.

I sit, curled into a ball on my kitchen floor. The cats cautiously approach me, attracted by my crying but scared of it at the same time. I was scared too. If I could go just one hour. One hour without hurting myself maybe I could make it all go away. My eyes burn holes into the clock on the stove as I watched the minutes slowly tick by. One hour became two, two became three.

I don't know when I fell asleep or even how I had made it into my bed that night. I was woken by the shrill sound of my phone's alarm at the unforgiving hour of eight in the morning. I had a mandatory work meeting to go to. I have to put on my happy face and smile. A smile means that everything is okay.

I pass as human.

Following the meeting, I go straight into a lunch shift. My hands are shaking. I hide in the bathroom when I can, the walk-in cooler when it makes more sense and I get through it. I crack jokes with my guests and co-workers. I'm a normal human. It's fine.

Everything's fine.

Sometimes that's what depression is. It's fake smiles and laughter. It's cracking jokes and saying "I'm fine." Depression, anxiety, panic isn't always easy to spot. It's even harder to talk about. There is so much stigma behind mental illness that people suffering are afraid to talk about it. I'm afraid to talk about it. To divulge the darkness that is sitting just below the surface. There's the fear of rejection. The fear of being brushed off. The fear of being "too dramatic." Of being told it's all in my head. Being told to get over it.

Why can't you just get over it? Just relax? Just stop? Do you have any idea how many times I've said that all to myself? It doesn't work like that.

When you are depressed. When you are having an anxiety or panic attack. When all of this is happening to you, you have no control over your thoughts, they have taken control of you and you are fighting a war against yourself. Do you have any idea how exhausting this is?

My memory from the next 24 hours is spotty at best. I was losing time. Functional but operating on autopilot. I was sitting in the waiting room at the Florida Hospital in Orlando when I called out of work on Sunday. I had no idea what my plan was at that point but I knew that going to work wasn't an option for me. I honestly had no idea if the hospital would let me leave once I talked to somebody about what was happening.

"Tell me about what you're feeling Josh."

"I'm feeling everything and nothing. I just want to scream and cry and just be angry at everything and I don't know why."

"Do you want to hurt yourself?"

I choke on the words but they come with almost no hesitation, "I do."

There is a pause, a heavy silence sitting in the air between the two of us. I take a deep breath and start again.

"I do, but I don't. It's there, that feeling. I want the pain, you know? That makes no sense but it does. I want to feel it."

"Do you want to die?"

I laugh sob. That's a thing. I did it. It's a thing.

"The angry, sad side of me does. The irrational part. The depression. But my rational brain doesn't. It wants to be alive for the stupidest most rational reasons. Does that even make sense?"

"Walk me through it. Give me an example."

"My cats. I can barely find people reliable enough to take care of them while I'm out of town, who on earth is going to take care of them if something happens to me?"

I spent a good chunk of the day at the hospital. I had turned my phone off after I called out of work and it was surprisingly refreshing to be disconnected, even for a short while. I was eventually allowed to go home.

I was honestly anticipating a psych-hold.

Depression lies.

Depression will lead you to believe some many things that aren't true and once it gets a hold on you, it doesn't let go easily. I know that there are people that love and care about me. There are friends I can lean on and talk to. I know I have that support system.

Depression tells me I don't. Anxiety tells me I'm a burden.

They are liars.

Sometimes it's just too hard to recognize it. To see through the haze, the curtain that these two will throw over your eyes. Sometimes they work to lead you to believe that there is just one path when in reality you've reached a fork in the road.

Depression is a lying bitch. Anxiety is it's best friend. The two are a wonder duo.

I hate them.

Monday morning I called out from work from that same waiting room. Was it going to be another long day at the hospital? All I knew is that I had used every ounce of my being to be in this moment and it was all the strength I had to be there.

"How are you feeling today?"

I take a genuine moment to ponder this question, "I feel empty. Well, not empty but numb... I feel blank."

"Blank?"

"Blank."

I go home and watch a stupid movie. I laugh more than I probably would have under different circumstances. It was the laughter of someone who just wanted to be happy. I think that's why Hollywood makes stupid movies.

Thanks for that. Thank you Zac Efron and Adam DeVine for starring in said movie.

Tuesday morning I went back to the hospital to speak to the doctor that had been assigned to me, trying really hard not to think about how much this was all going to cost me when it was over.

"How are you feeling today?"

"My version of human."

Close enough.

I really wish I had some answers or solutions to offer here as I bring this chapter to a close, but I don't. Each of us is fighting our own battles and everybody's is different. My anxiety and depression are not yours and they never will be.

I do know that I applaud everyone who goes out there every day and fights those battles. Sometimes that just means getting out of bed just to move to the couch. Sometimes that is all you have the energy for and that's just fine.

If all you did today was manage to hold yourself together then I applaud you. I applaud me.

That's allowed.

til it happens to you

Let me start by discussing the many ways that I have worked towards procrastinating the writing of this chapter. In the last 48 hours I have cleaned my entire house from top to bottom. I'm talking hardcore cleaned. I've lived here for almost four years and I'm fairly certain that this is the cleanest this place has ever been.

When I wasn't cleaning, I took the time to meal prep for the first time in months. I reorganized my closet (which really means that I made a massive mess in my closet, realized I was in over my head and closed the door in an effort to pretend it never happened). I wrote blog posts, I ran useless errands and now I have slapped a mud mask on myself because I know it means that in 30 minutes I need to take a break to wash it off.

I don't want to write this chapter.

But I have to.

I'm going to.

This story has never been told. It's something I have kept to myself for 16 years. My family knows nothing about it. I never talked to my friends about it. The only people that know about this were the ones directly involved and those it was reported to.

Until very recently I had forgotten all about it.

That might not be right. I don't think I forgot. I think I chose not to remember. It's one of those things, those moments you let slip away and bury deep into the dark abyss of your mind and hope against all hope that you never have to deal with it again.

But here we are.

Deep breath.

Continue.

I was 16 years old.

At this point in my life, I was out of the closet. Granted, I wasn't waving the rainbow flag and bursting glitter from my fingertips but I had come out to myself and was starting to let the people in my life in on the secret. Thanks to Gary, everyone at work already knew. I'd be mad about being ousted en mass but it really meant less work for me so I let bygones be bygones.

During the time when I was having issues with Gary's harassment, one of the older night cashiers, Stuart, pulled me aside as we were closing the store for the night. Try as I might, I don't remember the specifics of the conversation but I do know what the end result was. Stuart came out to me and offered himself as an ally.

I accepted, thankful not to be alone. I had love and support at school but work was one place it seemed to be missing. Now, it felt a little bit better.

Stuart was somewhere in his late 30's or early 40's and worked nights in the store in the customer service booth. I don't remember him being overly talkative but he wasn't lingering, quiet in the corner either. Aside from the manager, he was the oldest person on at night so he existed on the outside of our teenage nonsense.

He might have had kids? Maybe he had been married at one point? I have a pretty great memory but when it comes to this, when it comes to Stuart, there's nothing but darkness.

Part of me wants it to stay that way.

Deep breath.

Continue.

I have to issue a disclaimer of sorts before I can continue. I feel no ill-will towards the management at the store for how this situation was handled. Not then did I want to press charges or involve the authorities nor do I care to now. Back then I was a kid, I wanted it all to go away. I didn't want to be a burden. My management found themselves in a tricky situation. I'm next to positive they had never faced it before and it was alien territory.

There are no winners in this story.

I will admit that, in looking back, there are aspects in how this was handled that I'm not happy about but hindsight is 20/20. I know more now than I did back then. Back then I was young. I was scared. Back then I had just wanted it all to go away. Would I go back and do things differently? I don't know.

Deep breath.

Continue.

It was a Saturday. Another store in the company was short-staffed and needed cashiers. I had recently been promoted and my services were offered along with Stuart's. I didn't have my license yet so Stuart met me at our store and I rode with him to our sister store for an afternoon of work.

It was an interesting experience for sure as we quickly learned that, while in the same family, each store had its own little quirks and rules. By the end of my tenure with the company, I would have worked in each of the six stores in the chain, which is certainly something that helped me grow as an employee and a leader.

It was on the ride home that it happened.

I've gone back and forth about whether or not to go into specifics. I first wrote everything down in my notebook. Then I burnt the pages. As sat and typed them all out in the wee hours of the morning. Typed them right into this document. Then I deleted it.

Remembering that car ride felt exactly like those moments in a movie. You know, when a character has lost their memories and suddenly it all comes flashing back to them in random clips. Until right now, it always bothered me that they could see themselves in the flashbacks. They shouldn't see that. They should see things from their perspective, not the audience's.

But I can see myself sitting in Stuart's car. I can hear all the things that he said to me. I can see myself trying to move away from him, from his hands. I can see myself freezing in that moment. Unable to talk. Unable to move. Unable to stop what was happening.

So many times, when it comes to dangerous situations, people want to talk about the fight or flight response. They don't mention the third one. The freezing. It's a natural response in the face of trauma but no one talks about it.

I'm going to talk about it because for so damn long I felt ashamed that I didn't fight. Outside of moments like this it is so easy to talk about how brave you would be, how you would kick someone's ass if they ever tried to do something like that to you. But then you find yourself in that moment and everything you thought you would be loses ground to fear and shame.

It would be the better part of two weeks before I went to management. Working with Stuart had become unbearable. I didn't want him talking to me. I didn't want him looking at me. I didn't want him anywhere near me.

I requested the meeting with my manager and the company's operations manager. I couldn't just request not to work with someone without reason so I had no choice but to lay it all out for them. Realistically, I gave them the water-down version. Just enough information to justify not wanting to be on shift with him.

As a 16-year-old I had no idea how to handle the situation. I was terrified.

I can't help but look back and wonder now if my managers were just as scared. Just as confused. This was unfamiliar territory for all of us which is why I can't help but forgive them for getting it wrong. They didn't know better. This was a small, family-owned, company. Our HR guy was really just there to make sure everyone got their vacation pay and had the right amount of hours to maintain their insurance.

I don't think he was ever involved in this.

I told them I simply didn't want to work with Stuart anymore. I never wanted to see him again.

I left the office shaking.

The next time I worked I was called into the office and given the follow-up to their conversation with Stuart. They confronted him on what had happened and they told me that he opted to leave the company.

Fine by me.

But it was a lie. They lied to me.

It wasn't until sometime later that I learned that Stuart had been transferred to another store. The same store that the two of us had gone to work on that Saturday afternoon. It was closer to home for him and, more importantly, it was nowhere near me.

Everyone was happy.

Was everyone right in their actions? Not at all.

I let it go. I was away from Stuart and that was what mattered to me. I was hurt and betrayed by the fact that I was lied to but that was nothing compared to what had happened so I just let it go.

After graduating high school I was promoted and became a night manager for our store. I was always looking for more to learn and more opportunities so I was utilized company-wide and brought it to work at other stores as a manager to help cover vacations and last-minute callouts.

During my freshman year in college, I was called in to work as a closing manager in THAT store. I honestly didn't even think of Stuart when I got the call and agreed to go in and cover. He actually didn't cross my mind at all until two of the younger cashiers were talking about him.

I don't remember all the specific details but I know that Stuart had invited them to his house. I was instantly flooded with all of those memories from years before. The fear, the pain, the betrayal. I tried my best to warn the two of them against being alone with Stuart, especially in his home. I played it off as casually as I could.

Sitting here now thinking about those moments, I wish I had maybe done or said more. I don't know if they ever went.

I hope they didn't.

Deep breath.
Continue.

"I'm so mad at myself for not doing more."

It's a rare, cool night in Orlando. I'm sitting with my friend Kevin at a restaurant in Disney Springs. For the first time in 16 years I've said any of this out loud. First time I've told this story to anyone outside of the small circle of people who knew what happened.

"There is absolutely no reason why you should be mad at yourself. You did nothing wrong. You are the victim."

I don't know why but I never really thought of it that way. While it was all happening, I felt like I had done something wrong. I never told my mom or Henry because I felt like I would get in trouble. Henry, given his views, would have told me that I had it coming. Mom would have flipped out.

As a young kid still struggling with his sexuality, I was scared about being thrown into the limelight with such a scary situation. I was scared about having to recount it over and over again to my parents, my family, my friends, the police and god only knows who else.

At 32 years old, I'm still terrified to be writing this all down.

Deep breath.
Continue.

In the few months since this has all come back to me, I have spent a lot of time on the internet searching for some sort of insight, some fantastic bit of advice that I could offer up.

I've got nothing.

What I've found is that each and every survivor's story is different as are their ways of dealing with the trauma. I am finding myself in entirely new territory. All those years ago, I dealt with all of this by burying it deep and working very hard to forget all about it.

Now comes the question of where do I go from here?

I might not have been ready to face all of this at 16 years old but here I am, ready to talk about it, and I have. For me, sometimes, talking through things is the best way for me to deal with them. Since having that first conversation with Kevin, I've felt like a great weight has been lifted off of my shoulders. I had taken the first steps to getting it all out there, to writing this chapter.

Talking about it is often the first step and the most difficult. Saying it out loud makes it real. What's important is that you do it all on your terms, your timeline. If you don't want to talk about it, don't talk about it. When you do, go at your own pace.

What I love about talking with Kevin about sensitive subjects is that he never pushes, he lets you take your time and never makes you say more than you're comfortable with.

Find your Kevin.

It's okay to let it all out in small bits. If talking isn't for you, writing it out, draw it, sculpt it. Whatever it takes to help work through whatever it is that you are feeling. If you choose to talk to your parents or the police, be sure to tell them everything that you can remember. No matter what wrong-doing you think you may have done, nothing is worse than what was done to you.

It's not your fault.

A small part of me wonders how much of my life, my relationships, would be different if I had done more. I can wonder all I want, but it's not going to help. That's not what any of this is about. I'm not looking back to move backwards. This is all about moving forward.

Healing isn't always easy and for everyone it's different and a good chunk of the time, it never happens as fast as you'd like.

It's not a sprint, it's a marathon.

Some are faster and others are slower. We finish in our own time.

hands

Where were you?

That's always the question isn't it, when something major happens in the world? Where were you when it happened?

For most of the events that occurred in my early life, I don't quite remember all the details but I remember the events and the impact they had on the world. The Oklahoma City bombing. Princess Diana's death. The Columbine High School shooting. OJ Simpson.

Granted, I don't remember much about OJ Simpson other than I was at a friend's house when his brother came running outside where we were playing and screamed, "The Juice is running!" which, to me, was odd because juice belongs in the fridge.

From there, I remember we were all obsessed with a white Bronco for a while and I know that for some reason OJ Simpson is now the reason why we have Kardashians. My aunt Darlene's husband was obsessed with the case and for the summer we lived with them that's all we would hear about for months right up until the verdict was read on October 3, 1995.

For most of my early adult life, that big question revolved around the September 11th attacks and it's still a point of conversation today. Not too long ago I was discussing that day with a friend.

I first learned about the attacks when I walked into my history class that morning. I had been in my Project Adventure class first period and had been outside when the first plane struck the towers. When I entered the history room and saw the smoke billowing out of the World Trade Center on the TV my first, out loud, reaction was, "cool, we're watching a movie today!"

Ignorance is bliss.

I was quickly filled in on what was happening and we spent the remainder of the period sitting in shocked silence as the second plane struck and the two towers inevitably fell. The rest of the day was spent shuffling between classes simply to sit and watch the news. I remember my math teacher attempting to hold routine and told us that she'd leave the TV on but muted and we would have our lesson.

That didn't work out for her.

During lunch TV carts were rolled into the cafeterias and we continued to watch as rescue efforts slowly began, and the news broke of the plane crash in Philadelphia and another at the Pentagon.

I went to work that afternoon and spent every free minute in the meat department where they had a radio playing the news. I remember one of my co-workers who had just moved to town from New York City having to leave because she was so upset. Her face as she walked down one of the aisles after clocking out is something I won't forget. That whole day is one I won't forget as long as I live.

When it came to the September 11th terror attacks, I felt the same pain, fear, loss and heartache that swept the country. At the same time, I felt a disconnect. At the time, New York City was a place I had never been to and it only existed to me in TV shows and movies. To this day I have still never been to Washington DC outside of the airports and I shared no connection to anyone on the flights leaving Boston. I was safe in my world, in my bubble.

But then that bubble burst.

Monday April 14, 2013 was just another day for me. I was working as a box office supervisor for the

Aquarium in Boston and the day was anticipated to be slow on account of the marathon taking place across town and sure enough, it was.

The morning went by at a glacial pace but the city was alive with the energy of the day's events. You could feel the excitement in the air. At this time I wasn't one for running for fun, much less running 26 miles so I didn't put too much thought into the event. That's not to say I wasn't supporting my friends who were out there running their nipples raw but it wasn't for me.

When the bombs went off at the Boston Marathon finish line, I was down in the box office chatting with the cashiers. There were no visitors in sight and we were cracking jokes and discussing tales of crazy customers and whatever else came to mind.

Mark, a supervisor from another department called me on the radio and requested my location. He showed up outside the ticket booth almost instantly and motioned for me to join him outside. I was still laughing when I exited the booth to see what he needed.

"There was a bombing at the marathon finish line," he said once the door was shut and we were out of earshot of the cashiers.

The smile left my face. I could feel my heart drop and the blood seemed to leave my body. I could feel it leaving. I felt blank.

All at once a million questions came running through my mind. The aquarium had a team running the marathon and we had friends at the finish line. The blank feeling was quickly replaced by pure dread, terror and panic. All feelings I couldn't have in that moment because I was the one that had to turn around and let my staff know what was going on. I had to be calm for them.

Shortly after the news of the bombing broke the decision was made to close the aquarium. This involved having to clear the building and offering refunds to upset and confused visitors.

My co-supervisor helped with refunds in the main building while I went across the plaza to our IMAX theatre. I had to announce to the entire theatre what was going on. I kept my voice steady but my hands were shaking.

Once we were done clearing the theatre, I made my way back over to the main building but was stopped by a visitor who was leaving the aquarium. They were from another country and were upset that they were being made to leave. They felt that it was ridiculous that we were closing early and that the whole city was overreacting.

I calmly explained that a large part of the decision to close came from the city of Boston out of concern for large tourist destinations. Another major deciding factor from the Aquarium's standpoint was that the city was going to be shutting down public transportation and a large majority of the Aquarium's staff and volunteers relied on this to get home.

"That is the most selfish thing I have ever heard," the woman scoffed.

In a show of shear professionalism and quality customer service, I simply walked away. At this point we had no news of our friends in the race and at the finish line and I really didn't care about someone's vacation being ruined because we were closing what was really just two hours early, maybe even less than that.

Cell service was non-existent at this point as towers was overloaded. I couldn't get text messages to send or make calls. I used my office phone to call my sister and let her know I was okay and leaving the city soon.

My train ride home was a terrifying blur of confusion and fear. My commute was on the Blue Line which took my train right through the airport station where state police were out in full force. There might have also been National Guardsmen. My stop, Wonderland Station at the end of the line, was crawling with state troopers armed with massive guns.

As time passed that night we slowly got new about our team, our friends and their families. Everyone was okay.

The week played out in slow motion. I was scheduled to speak at a school in New Jersey on the 15th and 16th. They offered to reschedule but I stuck with the agenda, eager to get out of the city. I don't remember much from the workshops but I remember the students being a wonderful and supportive audience.

I returned to the Aquarium on Thursday to find that attendance was virtually non-existent. The entire city of Boston felt quiet and broken. A polar opposite of how this had felt in the early hours of that Monday morning.

Friday, April 19th was nothing short of a strange blur for me. I didn't have cable and never listen to the radio so I started my day ignorant to the ongoing manhunt and the shootout that had taken place in the early hours of that morning. My commute was thwarted by the subway not running and the woman at the parking station offered no explanation about why the trains weren't coming, just simply turned me away from the parking garage.

I had an email from the Director of Visitor Experience on my phone that simply asked that anyone that could get into the city to work to please do so. I wasn't thrilled about having to drive into the city but it looked like I didn't have any other choice.

I made the drive, baffled at the lack of traffic. Not once did I think to turn on my radio. It wasn't until I got to the office that I learned what was going on. The entire city of Boston and the surrounding communities were on lockdown.

There was a lot of back and forth about whether or not the Aquarium would open for the day but the decision was finally made that we would be keeping the doors closed. After a couple hours of getting in touch with staff and tying up loose ends, I went home.

I decided to occupy myself with some errands that I needed to run. It was my way of not having to think about the madness taking place just a few miles away. Grocery shopping, getting gas, running to the bank, and returning something to Target- all normal things. I wanted normal.

While sitting at a red light to turn into the mall plaza chaos broke out all around me. A police car appeared almost out of nowhere with sirens and lights blazing. Within seconds more police cars had arrived and blocked the intersection and the officers were out of their cars, guns drawn. They were pointed at a man I hadn't seen standing in the bushes near a Dunkin Donuts just a few feet away from my car.

An officer banged on my car window, telling me to duck down. I was paralyzed with fear and don't remember if I had complied or not. Then it was all over, ending as quickly as it had begun and I was motioned to move on from the intersection and carry on with my day as if this was all totally normal, like this kind of thing happened every day.

It took another police officer banging on my driver's side window and telling me to move along to snap me out of a daze. I was shaking all over and could barely focus on driving. I got myself into the Target parking lot and sat for a long time before I felt I could trust myself to move.

I finally decided to turn on the radio and try to gain come clarity as to what the hell was going on around me. It was right about this time that there was a lot of confusion about what vehicle the younger Tsarnaev was driving following the shootout the night before. The news was reporting that the police were currently looking for a Honda Civic. There I was, sitting in my Honda Civic.

Right around this time, my brain gave up. I went into autopilot and managed to drive myself to the nearby Barnes and Noble where I took a seat and decided to pretend like the rest of the world simply didn't exist. As I sat there, my phone started to buzz. Not done with me yet, the universe decided to deal one last blow.

A friend of mine from college that I hadn't spoken to in some time was on the other end. The news had released the name of the MIT officer that has been killed in the shootout with the bombing suspects. Sean Collier, a classmate from Salem State.

I had known Sean only in passing as we were both active in the Salem State community, taking part in club activities. At one point the two of us had to attend a student government meeting to request additional money for our group budgets. We weren't friends but he was a classmate, a human being, and an innocent victim.

The news hit me hard and I found myself in a state of shock. I called my friend Nina and walked her through the insanity that had been my day. I don't remember much of the conversation but Nina is always the best in times of craziness. I ended up sitting in the bookstore for some time. Just sitting. After a few hours I worked up the nerve to drive home.

That night I decided to stream the press conference turned grand finale. I joined the world in watching as it all came to an end. Well, as we all spent an insane amount of time looking at a boat. You could feel the city breathe a sigh of relief as it all ended and the official word came through that the final suspect was in custody. I could hear people cheering in the streets as I went to bed that night. The next day at work, you could feel the electricity in the air. We were safe.

At 2:00am on June 12, 2016 I was crawling into bed after a fun evening hosting game night at my house, unaware that just a few miles away tragedy was playing out in what would become the largest mass shooting (at the time) in the history of the United States and the deadliest terror attack since September 11, 2001.

I woke up a few hours later to the sound of my phone going absolutely insane. News of the shooting had gotten out and friends from back home in Boston as well as in Orlando we calling and texting to see if I was okay.

Facebook's safety check feature was a godsend during the next few hours as it allowed for a quick and easy way to let others know I was safe and for others to do the same. It had its limitations though and there were still many people we hadn't heard from. There were people that I wasn't friends with on Facebook. People that hadn't checked in. People who weren't answering their phones.

My anxiety was through the roof as I tried to get ready for work and carry about my day. To find out that something like this has happened in the town I call home and then try to carry on like normal is a lot easier said than done. This was an attack on my community. Both the city of Orlando and my LGBTQ+ brothers and sisters.

I tried very hard to stick to my routine. I made my usual stop at Starbucks where I ordered my usual drink and breakfast and tried my best at my usual banter. When you suffer from anxiety and PTSD, routine is best. Routine helps you feel in control, like you have power. I didn't though, I had none of those things.

I called Nina while I made my short drive to work at the restaurant. She was one of the many that had texted me and, while I had already responded to her, I needed a familiar voice on the phone. I needed to feel grounded. I tried so hard to stay calm on the phone but I was falling apart. I was on the verge of a panic attack and doing everything I could to stay calm and together but it wasn't happening.

I am beyond thankful for my co-workers and managers for not faulting me for not being able to make it through my shift. I tried so hard to stay strong, to be brave, to keep it together but I couldn't do it. The fear of not knowing, the exhaustion of trying to put on a happy front when inside I was crumbling, it was all too much.

I was offered the chance to leave but I refused out of my ridiculous work ethic. I couldn't abandon my shift. My friend Taylor stopped by to check up on me and I asked for a few minutes to step outside to talk to her. During this time my manager, Erin, made the call that my shift was over. She knew better than me that it wasn't in the cards for me to stick around. I'm grateful for her and for that decision.

Taylor came home with me that afternoon and we sat on my couch and ate Chipolte while watching Disney movies. What else was there to do? We sat and waiting, both constantly checking social media for any sort of news, good or bad.

That night Kevin stayed over, both of us in a heightened state of anxiety and not wanting to be alone. We sat up and talking until the darkest hours of the night had passed. He slipped into a Benadryl coma while I sat up staring blankly at something on Netflix while obsessively refreshing the City of Orlando page where the names of the deceased were slowly being released.

I found myself in the same position where I'd been just three years earlier in the aftermath of the marathon bombings. The fear and frustration of not knowing what was going on, if friends were okay.

I took the following day off from work. Shortly after calling out, the first familiar name showed up on the list of those lost. Kevin and I went to breakfast and made a plan to meet up later at Animal Kingdom. I'm not sure why we chose that park but we did. I have to say that in the hardest of times, there is nothing more cathartic than watching the Festival of the Lion King. Theatre is escape and it's what we needed.

On June 12, 2016 I lost three friends. In reality, I lost 49 brothers and sisters and those losses will stay with me for the rest of my life.

Often times we refer to moments like these as wake up calls, a time when you are bitch-slapped with the harsh reality of life. It's not something that can be planned for or scheduled, it just happens. You don't have a say in when it comes or how it will affect the rest of your life. The closer to home it hits, the more it hurts.

When it came to 9/11, I felt the same pain, fear, loss and heartache that swept the country. I felt proud to be an American but at the end of it all, there was that disconnect. That sense of knowing that it all happened but I still felt safe and sound in my own little bubble.

When it came to the Boston Marathon bombings and the Pulse Nightclub shooting, it was a lot closer, far more real. In Boston I was just two miles away from the finish line. I had a connection to that place, to those people. The same in Orlando, my newfound home. Pulse was a safe haven for the LGBTQ+ community. A place where my friends went to have fun and let loose.

My bubble had burst.

In times like this, really in any great crossroad in life, there are always two options. You can get bitter or you can show them that you are better.

After 9/11 we all became more patriotic than ever. There was a shortage of American flags because we were all in a rush to display them proudly. We weren't about to let hate win.

That's what I have seen through all of this. I have seen what hate can do to a community. I have seen the pain and fear that hatred can bring.

But I've seen what love can do.

The plaza that housed the restaurant I worked in was often home to a blood donation bus and Sunday June 12, was no different. Only on this day, when I pulled into the lot, a massive line of people was waiting to donate. This was the scene all over Orlando and beyond, people waiting in line for hours to donate blood. I won't forget that sight for as long as I live.

That night, the Tony awards paid tribute to the victims. The cast of Hamilton performed sans firearms out of respect. Lin Manual Miranda gave a speech to remember, reminding us that "Love is love is love is love."

We saw the same solidarity following the marathon bombings. Runners, finishing the race, kept running to Mass General to donate blood. The world came together to show their love and support.

At no point did we let hate win.

We never should.

college kids

College is a bullshit lie.

I'm sorry that was aggressive, let me try that again.

College is a fucking scam.

Holy shit, I'm sorry that was harsh. I'm really trying here.

I didn't want to go to college.

By the time my senior year in high school rolled around, I was really over the whole idea of continuing to go to school for another four years. More so, the idea of paying for it was unfathomable. I hated it when it was free, I had a feeling the paid version wasn't going to make me feel a whole lot better. That and I really had no idea what my ambitions were when it came to my future.

I had been moving up at the grocery store and making good money. Well, what I thought was good money because I was young, stupid and didn't know any better. I was pretty content with the idea of becoming a store manager. I had become the youngest manager in the company and was fully prepared embrace my life in retail. I was comfortable in my little bubble, what more did I need?

I was told in no uncertain terms that I would be going to college. The option was either to go to college, move out or start paying rent. My mom's idea of rent was more than I would have been paying in the real world so it seemed cheaper to go to college. Or so I thought.

I am quite proud to say that I was accepted into 100% of the schools that I applied to. Granted I only applied to one school so my success rate could have easily been 0%. I followed my older sister's example and applied to Salem State College in nearby Salem, MA.

I feel inclined to note that the school changed status to a University right after I finally graduated. They told me I could order a new diploma to reflect this for just $50, I informed them that I had already spent enough money on the first one.

My initial instinct was to apply as a business major as I was pretty set on the whole grocery store thing. In a moment of clarity, I declared English as my major along with a secondary education concentration. I had always like the idea of being a teacher and I was already a bookworm so the whole thing seemed to fit.

The joy and excitement of being accepted into college was marred by my mom's inability to respect my privacy, a common theme during my teenage years. The acceptance letter came and she opted to open it for me rather than waiting for me to come home from work. She didn't even give me a chance to read it myself, she just tossed the opened envelope at me and told me I was in. Sure, I wasn't keen on going to college in the first place but I still would have enjoyed the thrill of opening my own acceptance letter.

My first year consisted mainly of core classes and was relatively uneventful albeit a lesson in just how useless 8am classes are. I managed to get mono in my first semester because, why wouldn't I? I honestly didn't even get it from anything exciting, it was merely the curse of going to concerts and sharing a water bottle that was being passed around the crowd by strangers. All that aside, I managed to do well and fell into college life.

The problem was that I had no idea what I was doing there or what I even hoped to gain from the experience. What I did know that being an English major was expensive because for some reason we couldn't be reading reasonably priced books in all of our classes, no, we needed to be reading the leather-bound, gold-leafed tomes of yore, which were printed on the skin of virgins with ink made from the tears of a newborn. I can really only assume this is why college textbooks were so damn expensive. I see you book industry, I see you.

At the end of my Freshman year I tagged along with a friend of mine to an audition for Human Action Theatre, an educational troupe that performed during the freshman orientations sessions. I had really enjoyed them at my orientation so I figured it'd be fun to give it a shot. I auditioned with a monologue that I made up on the spot figuring I had no real chance of getting in, but I did and my eyes were opened to a whole new world. A new, more expensive world.

I dove into the life of a theatre kid head first and never came up for air. I hadn't been on stage since sometime in Middle School and I found myself in love with it as I had been back then. The cast of Human Action Theatre (HAT as we called it) welcomed me with open arms and that summer was one to remember. I fell back in love with the stage and found myself yearning to be a part of that life again.

Rather than switching majors to a less secure field, I decided to err on the side of caution and stick with English but also add on a second major with Theatre. Now, you're probably wondering why I didn't minor in Theatre and save myself a butt-load of time, energy and money. I'm going to be honest, I graduated almost ten years ago and I'm sitting here wondering the same exact thing and I don't have an answer for you.

Wait, I do have an answer. I had no idea what I was doing and had no one to help point me in the right direction. You'd think my advisor would have been a help, but she wasn't. Nothing against her, I just don't think she was prepared for a student like me, who knew nothing about what their aspirations were and what they really wanted to do with college, their degree or their life. I chose a degree in English because I loved to read and added Theatre because it was something fun to do. What did I want to do with them? Not a damn clue.

This should have been a massive red flag for everyone involved, primarily me. I didn't have a plan and I was slowly but surely digging myself a massive financial hole in the form of student loans while I was trying to figure it all out. Pursuing a degree in English is freakishly expensive. For a single literature class I would end up dropping $500 on books alone. It's gotten a bit better for kids today because there's the option to rent books apparently but I'm old and we weren't offered that. Theatre classes weren't much better as those books on their own could be $150 or more.

I was taking out loans with reckless abandon because I had no idea what I was doing. This is where the American educational system is really taking an opportunity to screw over the population. First we are brainwashed into the idea of college because we're told that, without it, we won't get a good job to take care of our families and buy houses and have beautiful golden retrievers. Next, we are taught nothing about loans, credit, and taxes. To this day, I have no idea how to balance a checkbook and I use the "swipe and pray" method when it comes to using my debit card.

More so, I was taking care of myself. Following my freshmen year Henry kicked me out of the house and I was now in the position of not only working to pay for college but also to keep a roof over my head. I was working full-time at the grocery store, taking a full course load to maintain full-time status as a student, and trying not to fail at everything.

If this was the American dream then I had some questions about who's whiskey-addled delusions I was living in.

By time I walked across the stage to receive my diploma I was $60,000 in debt and had no idea what I was going to do with my life after my degree. I seriously walked across the stage humming "What Do You Do With A BA in English" from Avenue Q. Now, ten years later, I'm sitting here humming "It Sucks to Be Me" from the same show.

That's not to say that my time at school was a complete waste. Following my first summer with Human Action Theatre I applied to direct the group for the following year and was accepted. This was a role I held every year until I graduated and I couldn't be more grateful for the loveable group of weirdos I managed to assemble each year to teach the incoming freshmen about college life. People thought I was a psycho not only for how many times I returned to direct but for how seriously I took it all. I strove to find more purpose behind the show and bring a focus to the educational side of it. Sure, we were still ridiculous and over the top, but we taught lessons through the laughter and that was important to me.

Truth be told, my favorite part of my college life was my time spent in extracurricular activities. This is honestly where I felt like I was really accomplishing something and ended up learning more here than I did in the classroom. I really mean nothing against the wonderful faculty that tried to get information into my brain but, looking back, I realize that I was not meant for the classroom. I've always learned better by doing and experiencing rather than having information thrown at me. Throw me to the wolves and I won't come back leading the pack but I'll definitely have a learned a thing or two.

What I lacked in the ability to be a driven and focused student, I more than made up for in my ability to get involved on campus. After my first year with HAT I dove head first into campus activities. I found myself on executive boards for various groups including our Student Theatre Ensemble and Program Council. The latter being my absolute favorite. Program Council was responsible for some of the biggest events on campus including bringing in comedians, speakers and even the occasional build-a-bear because college was stressful and we needed fun.

As part of my theatre major we were required to work on department productions over the course of each semester. I assistant directed on two productions, one of which was the most intense production of Antigone ever seen in the history of theatre (in my opinion). I mean that in the best possible way. That, in and of itself, was a full-time job for everyone involved. The production was headed by Professor Celena Sky April who taught me more about life and leadership and art than anyone ever could have. I had worked with her the semester prior on a theatrical reading of Fahrenheit 451. All said and done I spent two solid years by her side making art that I was truly proud of not just for myself but for everyone involved.

This would be a good spot for you to stop and do some mental time math with me. I was going to school full-time, working full-time, held a place on a total of four executive boards, was involved in full-scale theatrical productions, and sometimes did my homework. If you're wondering when I slept, the answer is never. That's a lie, I took some pretty epic naps in the Program Council office when I wasn't hosting balloon sword fights or chastising my advisor Allie for eating an entire package of Oreos without even offering to share one.

But even with all of that, I still had no idea what I was doing and what direction I was supposed to be going in. My plate was full but I was still hungry.

"I regret going to college" is a statement that leaves my mouth quite often. I regret it because it was time and money that was lost learning that I had no clue. I still don't have an idea but I do know that I'll be paying student loans for what feels like the rest of my life.

I can see college being a powerful asset if you aspirations are to become a doctor, an educator, or a lawyer. When you're me and your aspirations can change weekly, sometimes hourly, it can seem like a massive waste and that's what it felt like to me. I was pressured by my family and society to go straight from high school into college without being given time to consider what would be best for me.

Had I wanted to stick to a path of becoming a teacher then I would have been on the right track, but I was quickly turned off to the idea when I saw just how convoluted it was to become a teacher. More than that, my chosen subject of English is a part of the standardized testing we've become so obsessed with and so much of what I would have been doing would be teaching students how to pass a test. A test, mind you, that does nothing to better serve students.

In Massachusetts we had the MCAS which is a test that I, to this day, hate with a burning passion. My hatred stems from the fact that the year I moved from California to Massachusetts while I was in high school was the first year that MCAS testing was implemented. I was livid mostly because in California, their standardized testing was done during the freshmen year. So I spent my entire first year of high school preparing for a test, which I passed with honors, only to spend another year learning to take yet another standardized test.

The days I spent doing classroom observations were what really did me in when it came to wanting to pursue teaching. I don't know if it was my timing or the universe was really trying to mess with me but it came during a time when teachers were reviewing for the upcoming testing. The kids were stressed, the teachers were stressed, and since I am an emotional sponge, I became stressed. I wasn't even taking the damn thing. When I was able to chat with the teacher during a free period she confided in me that it felt like all she was preparing the kids for was passing one single test.

This wasn't what I wanted from a career education and over the course of that particular semester I found myself pulling further and further away the idea of teaching. The final nail in the coffin was when I took a good look at the Massachusetts Tests for Educator Licensure practice tests. The first questions was so confusing and terrifying that I curled into a fetal position and cried for a while. I eventually looked over the whole test and couldn't help to think it was bullshit. Sure, I need a working knowledge of literature and whatnot to be able to teach but all this really was testing was my ability to parrot out information. Just because I knew the answers didn't mean I was going to be a good teacher. It was a damn MCAS for adults and I was having none of it.

I soldiered on through my secondary education minor because I wanted to make sure I had a fallback in life. A fallback from what, I still had no idea but Sallie Mae kept giving me loans and I kept going to school in the hopes of finding an answer. When I finally walked across the stage, six years after first setting foot on campus, I received a BA in English concentrating in creative writing and secondary education along with a BA in theatre concentrating in performance.

Remember a few chapters ago when I mentioned I was working in a restaurant? I may not be doing everything right but, damn it, I make a damn good living stereotype! I also maintain that my diploma is the most expensive piece of paper I will ever own. It's proudly displayed in a room in my house that I enter once every few months at best mostly to remind myself it's still there. The room, not the diploma. That thing gets stolen I can put an insurance claim on it. That's a $60,000 piece of paper.

Totally worth it.

high hopes

When I graduated from college I was greeted with a less than ideal job market. If ya'll remember, 2009 wasn't the greatest for the economy and no one was really hiring. On the same vein, I had no idea what my actual plans were beyond knowing that six months after I was done with schooling, Sallie Mae was going to be coming for her money. I was still at the grocery store at this time so I had an income but I was starting to feel like I had outgrown that life. I was the only person working there with a college degree and it's not that I felt that I was better than anyone, but I had the feeling that it was getting to be time to move on.

At school I had fallen in love with Human Action Theatre and it was something that defined me during my time at Salem State. I loved being a part of the show because it offered the opportunity to welcome in the new freshmen to the crazy world of college. I also loved being able to teach which was still a passion despite being turned off by the formal educational setting.

The show itself is comprised to a series of comedic and dramatic vignettes written by the cast about college life. We were tasked with touching on certain topics deemed important by the college to educate the incoming freshmen. These included serious topics like drugs, alcohol, sex, suicide and depression, self-image and sexual identity. We also had comedic moments like a 12 Days of Christmas parody entitled "The 12 Days of College" that was the highlight of every show.

We had free range with the show which was a blessing and curse, depending on how you looked at it. Nothing was off limits including language. One of my favorite moments during a show came in the middle of the 12 Days of College song. There is a diva fight between two of the actors. One cast member, Kerrin Rhudda, wanted the part of "Day 5" in an effort to really show off vocally. She is miffed at Andy Scannell who got the part instead and keeps interrupting him. In a moment that was completely unscripted and a surprised to everyone, including Andy, he sings out

"Just take the part you cunt!" to the tune of "five golden rings!"

I don't know if you've ever seen twelve people simultaneously die on stage before but it surely happened in this moment. I was laughing so hard I'm fairly certain I peed a little and it took us all a solid minute to regain composure and continue on with the show. The crowd of freshmen were living for the nonsense.

While Andy certainly wasn't in trouble for the vulgarity, as the show's director, I was given the very strong suggestion that it shouldn't happen again. Andy being Andy took that as a challenge to sneak the now forbidden c-word into the show in other ways. Most directors would probably be annoyed by this but I respected his ability to stand up for what he believed in even if it was calling Kerrin a bad word. She probably deserved it anyway.

By both Andy and my final year with HAT in 2009, the new advisor for the show, my Program Council advisor Allie, expressly forbade Andy from saying that vile word. If you missed the loophole we sure as hell didn't. She told Andy he couldn't say it. Now, in the interest of full disclosure, no one uttered the c-word on stage once that year. Instead I snuck it in another way.

For the 2009 year the theme of orientation was "Making a new Mii" based on videos games. I was mildly bitter because I had unsuccessfully pitched the idea of "Taking it to the Next Level" based on old-school Nintendo but the higher ups felt it was too out-dated. So I themed HAT to it instead. The overall through line for the show was that Andy and I were two friends sucked into a video game where we travelled through lessons surrounding self-image, racism, STDs and the like.

At one point during the show, Andy and I are going a separate ways after a scene and I yell after him, "Alright dude, see you next Tuesday."

Cue audience laughter and one slightly miffed, albeit impressed Allie. I'm fairly certain she outwardly yelled at me from the audience that she was going to kill me. That's probably not true but she was definitely sending those vibes my way.

I'd like to say that this is the only time I've kind of said a bad word in front of an audience but I once accidently said "twat" in front of a group of high school students. I heard it leaving my mouth as it was happening and purposely stumbled over my words in an effort to mask it. No one seemed to notice and no one said anything to me so I'm fairly certain I got away with it. I also have never been invited back to that school so that might be why. Hard to tell.

Needless to say my time with HAT remains some of my best memories from college. As I was the first student to direct the show for multiple years, I recast a lot of the same people year after year while still being sure to add new blood each summer. We built and amazing family and my time with them is something I wouldn't trade for the world.

In my final year at Salem State, resulting in my final year with HAT, it was my friend and cast mate Bobby Savage who bluntly stated one day during rehearsal, "you know Josh, you can't just do HAT for the rest of your life!" The is one of my favorite things about Bobby. He's blunt and he's real and has an amazing talent at keeping people grounded. His comment was in jest but he had a point.

Or did he?

It was during my time with HAT that my career as a professional educational speaker was born. During the 2005 sessions we were asked to touch upon internet safety as part of the show. Facebook was still a baby at this point and was just for college students. A feature of the site at the time was that you were able to link your class schedule and be connected to your classmates. Our advisors wanted us to stress personal safety when it came to sharing this information.

For the scene I had the pleasure of playing the stalker while my friend Mandy played my unsuspecting victim. I, apparently, have a knack for playing creepy. Nothing to be proud of really but it's landed me some great roles in both movies and even a web series that never made beyond tables reads. The scene was short but effective and we rounded it out with statistics surrounding an increase in stalking cases on college campuses with the advent of social media.

I truly loved the work we did with Human Action Theatre. It gave us all the opportunity to not only be on stage performing, but to educate our new classmates. The show was written by us and on our terms. Along with all of that, we had an insane amount of fun from rehearsals to our annual cast trip to Six Flags to performing the show.

When it came to thinking about next steps in life, I couldn't help but think back to Bobby's remark. Why couldn't I do HAT forever? I mean, the show experience as I knew it couldn't be recreated elsewhere in our way of performing it. Our show was specific to Salem State because we knew Salem State.

I thought back to my first year performing with the group. I had written a monologue based on my audition that was about self-worth and not judging a book by its cover. The director put the monologue at the top of the show and every time I performed it, it was electric. More so, I was the very beginning of the show. I had the job to not only to educate but to sink the hook into the audience to keep them on board with us for the rest of the show.

From Human Action Theatre, I learned how to capture an audience with what could easily be boring material. How does a group of twenty-something's make statistics about STDs entertaining? Do a dance to Britney Spears "Toxic"! Teach a group of 18-year-olds about academic dishonesty? Perform it like an over-acted PSA from the 80's. Educate and entertain was the name of the game.

I knew I had the power and stage presence to take hold of an audience on my own. I may not have been a great actor but I was an engaging storytelling. I knew how to combine humor with sincerity and to create tension and a spark. Sure, I was used to performing as part of a group but I could very well strike out on my own. Couldn't I? Could I make performing and educating a full-time career? Could I make Human Action Theatre my life?

The groundwork had already been set without me even realizing it in early 2009. Normally HAT only performed during orientation sessions in the summer and was dormant through the school year. During winter break one of the advisors reached out to me and asked if we would be able to put together something for Salem State's Peace and Social Justice Week. We agreed and put together an entirely new show in just three weeks. It was a rush!

I started playing with the idea of HAT doing just more than orientation, wondering what could more could we accomplish with our talents. We had the sketches, we had the ambition, why not use it? Over spring break in March of 2009, I developed on an existing program created by one of our advisors about internet safety into what essentially amounted to a one-man show. I reached out to local high schools offering the program free of charge to give it a try. One took me up on the offer.

The event went over better than expected and I kept this in the back of my mind as I went about life. When the semester ended HAT was hard at work for our summer shows. At the time I was planning on diving back into academia for a third degree in Communications because, again, I had no idea what I was doing and I had found a comfort zone in Salem State. The universe had other plans. I wasn't able to secure a loan and dropped the idea of returning to school.

So there I was. Out in the real world with two degrees, a crappy job market, and no idea what I wanted to do. I also had an internet safety program. Why not doing something with it? I started advertising the program around, first to schools in my area and then slowly out to schools all over New England and eventually out to a good chunk of the east coast. The program began to pick up steam and soon I was working all over the country.

I had never really travelled much outside of bouncing back and forth between California and Massachusetts as a kid. One year in high school I went to Florida with a friend and her family but I had never done any travelling on my own. When my speaking engagements took me on an overnight trip somewhere, I often enlisted friends to come with me as I was terrified to go about it alone. I was so unsure how travelling was done that I actually drove everywhere. This lead to some pretty amazing adventures and my memories from my early days of working as a professional speaker are ones I will cherish for the rest of my life.

It wasn't until I did a ridiculously crazy drive from Boston to Tennessee that I realized I was unnecessarily exhausting myself and I decided to give flying to performances a try. I never had booked a plane ticket before, never rented a car, never stayed in a hotel by myself. I didn't have the slightest clue how it was done but I figured it out and soon I was an unstoppable force.

I spent a great deal of time studying other professional speakers, specifically those dealing in internet safety and eventually bullying. I saw what worked and what didn't and I learned just what kind of speaker I wanted to be. While I'll gladly dress business casual for a parent night or keynote presentation, I'm all t-shirts and jeans with the kids. Not because I'm trying to impress anyone but because I strive to just be real with them. Real Josh doesn't even own and suit and after leaving my job at the grocery store, I swore I'd never wear a tie again as long as I lived.

I scoffed at, and still do, being called a motivational speaker. I very much maintain that the energy, enthusiasm and sun shining disposition conveyed by motivational speakers beyond my abilities as an actor or even a human. If I even attempted to fake it, I would be ousted as a fraud immediately and I would lose the audience before I even had a chance to gain their trust. Realistically, I have no preferred title, just anything but motivational speaker.

In a weirdly roundabout way, I had found my path and I was able to have a job that brings me such joy that it's hard not to be passionate about it. Even on days when I'm jetlagged and frustrated about life, getting on stage in front of an audience and having the ability to make a difference in their lives is something that's hard to get mad about.

Not too long ago, Bobby found his way to Florida on vacation and I met up with him and his girlfriend at Epcot one afternoon. He had left Massachusetts as well and was living in New York with Andy and some other friends from our theatre days. I was thrilled to hear how well he was doing and he expressed the same for me. "You did it. You actually did it. It might not be HAT but you're doing it."

It might not be HAT and I may be doing it for the rest of my life, but yeah, I'm doing it.

save myself

November 22, 2017

It's the day before Thanksgiving and against my better judgment, I took a booking at a school in New York that would have me in airports on the busiest travel day of the year. It's been a tough year for booking schools so I wasn't really in a position to turn down work.

I flew in the day prior to the assemblies as I normally do and spent the better part of the day hold-up in a Barnes & Noble in Connecticut, parking myself in the café with a green tea and blueberry muffin, working on my revisions for all the chapters you've just gotten through reading. I also spent some time thinking about what I wanted to talk about with the students during the following day's programs.

The bones of my programs are pretty standard across the board: online safety, social media etiquette, and bullying prevention. Then there's the extra bits that I like to bring to the table. The moments of personal connection that really gets the audience in tune with the message and brings them to the edge of their seat.

A pin-drop moment.

It's never the same moment. I can have multiple audiences at the same school and that moment of pure connection can be different for each. Sometimes it's in an instant. The moment the spotlight is on me, I own the room. Other times it doesn't come until later, it takes a little more work to earn the trust of the audience. Sometimes it doesn't happen at all. These are the worst because there are no winners.

I was once hired to speak at a college in Pennsylvania and it was a nightmare from the moment I stepped foot on the campus. The woman that had initially contracted me had left the school for another job and I was treated more as an inconvenience than a guest. I was given all the wrong information by my new contact which made for a frustrating beginning. I was led to an auditorium already seated with a few hundred college students who clearly did not want to be there.

I absolutely despise having to get things set up while an audience is already in the room. It's horrifically awkward because there's a method to my madness. From what students see when they enter, to the introduction, everything. As a performer, having a set structure is important to my process which is why I can come across as somewhat demanding in my technical rider, the instructions on what I need. My demands.

I've shown up to schools who are completely and terrifyingly unprepared for a visitor. Once, I drove all the way to New Jersey from Boston in the middle of a snowstorm just to arrive at the school the next morning to discover that the organization that hired me never passed along that I was coming.

This has happened to me twice in ten years of speaking professionally and it's the absolute worst. It's always my biggest fear especially since I'm often travelling to places unfamiliar and far from home. For the record I was paid in full for both programs.

This school in New York, however, was a standout and a great way to end my 2017 tour year. I had spoken there before years ago and was thrilled to be invited back and they went above and beyond to make me feel welcome in their community. It means a lot to me when a school is prepared and more so when they make sure I know the location of the nearest Starbucks.

I started the day with a quick, abridged, session with 6th graders. It was shorter than I normally care for but still managed to be tons of fun. The day before a holiday break can be tough, especially since they were also on a half day but the kids were high energy and attentive. I was on a roll and I could feel it. It was going to be a great day.

The following session with the older kids went just as well, if not better. They were just as enthusiastic as the younger crowd and eager to have a good time. I was excited to wrap the day on a high note and leave them with some food for thought over the Thanksgiving weekend.

With any job you need those moments that re-energize you. Don't get me wrong, I love my job but the travel, early mornings and sometimes even the material can take a toll on me. It can burn even the best out. Then there are the days that remind me why I do it, that help me find that same amazing spark that I felt on day one.

That was this day.

The session itself was relatively routine in the grand scheme of things. I always know what I need to say but sometimes my stories and jokes will vary depending on the audience and my mood. If I'm running back to back sessions I tend to get sick of my own jokes so I change things up mostly to keep myself entertained. We got through the workshop and ended up with some time left over for a question and answer session. Often times I will purposely run out the clock and don't allow for Q&A because I either get zero questions and I have no choice but to dismiss the session earlier than administrators would like or I have to put up with completely asinine questions.

Examples include: "What's your favorite ice cream flavor?" (Ben and Jerry's Americone Dream or Cookie Dough) and "What kind of socks are you wearing?" (usually something with dinosaurs on them because I'm a five-year-old).

That wasn't the case today. The questions fired my way were smart, honest questions revolving around the topics we had discussed over the course of the assembly. This made my heart almost explode with happiness because it meant that they were engaged throughout the program and were eager to learn more. I was happy to oblige.

As we were wrapping things up I decided to take one last question. Fun fact about when I'm taking questions, if there are ten different people pointing wildly at you, there's a good chance I'm not going to call on you because it usually means something ridiculous is about to be thrown my way. I chose a young man who was sitting quietly with his hand raised.

"How many lives do you think you've saved by talking to students?"

Holy. Shit.

I had to take a moment to think about this. On one hand, there are countless emails and messages I have received from students over the years telling me that I changed their lives, I've inspired them, that I've made a difference in their lives. I've been told that my words have had a lasting impact and have encouraged others to stand up not only for themselves but for one another. I have been told that I have saved lives.

One story that I've told often, usually when speaking to educators, is that of a young man that I met while I was speaking at a small school in Texas. I remember this school because it had been something of a nightmare. I had been hired in by the technology coordinator who was a tad more liberal than his superiors were. When I arrived on campus, he brought me to meet the principal of the school for a quick chat as I often like to do before a program. It helps me get a feel for the school atmosphere, especially if any issues have been going on, I can address them in my own subtle way. Rather than discussing any issues, the principal had one request for the program.

"We're really excited to have you here and I just have one thing we want to avoid discussing," she started.

I was expecting her to ask that I either tone down or remove any bits about sexting. This is usually an iffy subject with some schools, especially in more religious areas. I'm so used to this, I have programs already on hand that have the topic removed so I can easily jump into it.

Instead she hit me with, "I just want to make sure you don't talk to the students about the queer kids killing themselves."

It wasn't a request to omit talk of suicide from the program. She didn't want me talking about gay people bullied or otherwise.

I was dumbfounded. I was shocked. I was down-right insulted. A part of me wanted to just get up and leave. I managed to keep my cool and just sort of smiled and nodded a little despite fighting the burning desire to jump down this woman's throat for being so terrible. She couldn't be bothered to come to the assembly so I couldn't be bothered to honor her request about avoiding talking about those damn bullied queer kids.

Following the program I noticed that aforementioned young man lingering on the periphery of the crowd that came to talk to me as everyone filed out of the gymnasium. He waited for everyone to leave until he approached. I could see he was building himself up to talk to me so I smiled and introduced myself properly, hoping to ease his nerves.

He kept starting and stopping, choking on his words. I found myself breaking one of my biggest rules when it came to interacting with students- I gave him a hug. He started crying.

"I'm scared," he managed after a moment.

Truth be told, I was scared for him. I had just gotten through telling him and all of his classmates that the adults in their lives had their backs and would be there for them through anything. For the first time in my career, I felt like a liar. Granted, I had only met the principal but she made me feel unsafe in her school and I was simply a guest there. I had the freedom to leave that school, leave that town, leave that state. This kid didn't. He was stuck in this small-minded school.

I'm happy to say that he had since graduated and is in college far, far away from that town, that school, that principal. We kept in touch over the years and though he had his struggles, he has made it through with flying colors. The summer after his freshman year in college, he came out to his family and it went well. He is safe, happy and loved.

This story crossed my mind as I stood in front of my audience in New York and I started to tell it but something made me stop. I thought about everything I had discussed with them that morning. I talked about the Pulse shootings, mental illness, depression and my anxiety. I talked about being bullied and how I worked to overcome and prove to the world that I was better.

"Right here, right now, each and every one of us has survived 100% of our bad days," I had told them during the program. "That's a pretty good track record if you ask me."

In an instant I thought back on all of that. I thought back on the almost ten years that I had spent travelling around the country having these conversations with students. I thought about how I had grown, and changed, and evolved over those years. Not just my programs but me as a person. How travelling and sharing with my audiences has helped me address things on a more personal level. I had learned that it was okay to talk about my mental illness, my depression and anxiety. That I was allowed to be human.

"There's something funny about having a job like mine," I start after taking a moment to really think about what answer I want to give. "I was told when I started speaking at schools that, statistically, I would only really reach 1% of each audience. It's nothing against me, but I was told that was the reality of people that speak professionally in schools.

Thankfully, I'm not a big believer in statistics. I like to think that I reach more than 1%. Maybe I do, maybe I don't but I'm going to go ahead and believe that everyone receives my message in their own way. I never get to know though. There's no way of measuring my success. Sure, teachers will tell me how wonderful it was, administrators will pass along my name in praise to other schools but when it comes to students, it's hard to tell.

So, I guess that answer to the question is, I really don't know. I mean, sometimes I will get emails from students telling me that I made a difference in their lives and that's always a great feeling. But I don't hear from everyone and that's okay too.

Here's what I do know. I may never have a tally on lives that I changed or saved but I know of one important one. My own.

Whenever I'm having a bad day, whether it's anxiety or depression showing their ugly faces, and I feel those bad thoughts creeping in, I think about the emails I have received. I think about the lives I know I've changed. I think about the difference I have made and want to continue to make. I think about the amazing feeling that I get when I stand in front of an audience, just like this, and have these empowering and inspiring moments.

I may never know the number of people I've reached or the number of lives I could possibly have saved, but I know that, if anything, I've been able to save myself."

I pause, the theatre is quiet. You can feel it all hanging there in the air.

"Sometimes you have to be your own superhero and if the only person you can save is yourself, that's just fine."

the long way around

I had life all figured out, as one does, at the ripe age of ten-years old. My friend Jared and I discussed it all at great lengths while sitting on the play sets of Gallagher Park on Pine Hill in Lynn, Massachusetts. As best friends we, naturally, were going to buy big houses right next door to one another, our wives would be the best of friends and so would our kids. Our houses were going to be connected by a tunnel so it'd be easy to go back and forth in the winter. We'd have jobs that made us rich and you'd better believe we have a pool, which is very important when you're ten.

Well, you know what they say about the best laid plans.

Actually, no. Sidebar. No one knows what they say about the best laid plans. I thought about this because it was easier than writing a book at the time. So often people will say, "whelp, you know what they say about the best laid plans" and you just shrug and nod like you have any idea what is going on. You don't, but god forbid anyone else knows that. So let me share what they say about those best laid plans. It stems from a poem written in 1785 called "To A Mouse" which was written by Robert Burns, supposedly after destroying a mouse's nest while plowing his fields.

"The best laid schemes of mice and men / go often askew."

So first off, we need to stop saying "best laid plans" and start saying "best laid schemes" because not only is it correct, but it sounds a lot cooler. We don't use the word "scheme" enough and I think that's a damn shame.

Back the schemes of my ten-year old self. They went pretty damn askew.

I did decided to look up Jared on Facebook, mostly for procrastination reasons. We didn't say friends after I moved from Lynn back to California. We did run into each other at Salem State once, neither realizing that we both went there. We had befriended one another on Facebook back then since it was the thing to do but apparently he got swept up in one of my many friend-list purges. He's married now and has a kid. Looks like he still may even be in Lynn.

Once upon a time, maybe, there was a prescription for how life went. A timeline we were all supposed to be following. You went to high school, maybe college, you got a job and settled down. You had a mortgage, a car payment, a family and a plan. There was a blueprint that we are all supposed to follow and that's just the way of the world. It's the path that my grandparents followed, it's the path that my parents followed and it's the path that I took one look at and said, "nah, I'm good."

I blame the internet.

Not in the way that the baby boomers blame the internet. Sure, the system has its faults and there's a good chance that Facebook helped Russia take over America, but the internet did something amazing for, not just me but, my generation. It opened our eyes to an entirely new world around us. Not even a new world, just THE world. The world at our fingertips and we weren't content to just let it be an image on a screen, we wanted it all.

In 2009, when I started speaking professionally at schools, I slowly but surely worked my way out of my comfort zone. As I travelled more and more, I grew less and less satisfied with my boring, safe job at the grocery store and after over a decade of working there, I gave my notice. The world was out there and it wasn't going to be found arguing about the cost of cucumbers, putting out lobster tank fires and mopping up the urine of the local homeless woman (all of these things happened during my tenure at that store and will likely fill the pages of my next book).

I left the grocery store in the summer of 2011 with the plan of making a full-time job of speaking professionally. As it was summer and schools weren't in session, I still needed an income so I took a seasonal position at the New England Aquarium. I had been volunteering there as an educator and loved it so I jumped at a chance to do more. It gave me a safety net and the schedule allowed me to build towards a fall of travelling the country and speaking to students, parents and more.

At the end of the summer I was offered a full-time position but respectfully declined as I wasn't willing to settle down. I loved the job but I wanted more and sitting still was not appealing to me. I had spent the summer filling my schedule with school visits all over the country, jumping at the opportunity to explore new and exciting places that I never would have thought to visit or probably wouldn't have been able to afford to. It was the dream I never knew I had.

The following summer I returned to the aquarium for the season in a new role as a supervisor in the box office and it was a blast. I will forever maintain that this was the greatest job I ever had. It was, at times, insane and people were often the worst but my co-workers were the best. The job was great for me because there was no predictability in it. No one day was the same and even when things were at their craziest it was never unbearable, we always seemed to come out of the other end of it laughing our asses off.

I have the say that the dynamic with my cohorts in the Aquarium Box Office was second to none. I'm eternally grateful for the manager, Gigi, who put up with my insanity with a smile and was easily one of my favorite people to talk to about everything and nothing all at the same time. My co-supervisors were the best. Della taught me how to fashion and Rachel was the little sister I never wanted. We were a family and we worked amazingly well together. I'm so damn thankful for them, you have no idea.

Come the fall I was back on the road with something of a twist. My seasonal position was extended so the full-time supervisors could take vacation time and the department was still covered. It didn't require me to be there full-time so I was happy for the extra money. Before we knew it, my season had been extended so much that I either needed to be cut loose or brought on as a regular employee. There was no question in my mind that I loved the job and the position was part-time and they only needed me the weekends. More importantly Gigi was willing to work around my touring schedule so long as I made myself available for the busier times of year and back to full-time for the summer season.

Just shy of twenty years after those swing-set conversations with Jared, I was living a life that I never could have imagined. Was I married? Nope. Kids? I had cats so that counts. Big house? Savings? Retirement? Job Security? None of it. But I had my life and I was happy with it despite being wildly outside the comfortable norms of the world.

Soon though, that familiar itch found its way into the back of my mind. Funny enough, I had found my way back to Lynn, Massachusetts. I had found a small one-bedroom apartment that I was completely in love with. The building had been a luxury-hotel at one point in time and had since been converted. The bathroom was miserable and the kitchen was laughably tiny but I loved the place. It fit everything about me and it was perfect. It didn't dawn on me until just now that fifteen years after leaving Lynn, I was back, living just over a mile away from my former Pine Hill home and that park where my life plans were made.

But that itch.

I had spent a large part of my life in Massachusetts and it was wearing on me. I loved and still love the city of Boston, the people and the culture but the winters were doing their best to drive me insane. Snow was my mortal enemy and I hated everything about it. I was yearning for something new, something different, something warmer.

Florida was calling my name. I had been taking regular trips there for some time to visit a friend from high school who was working for Disney. She introduced me to Disney World, my first time seeing Cinderella's Castle was when it was all lit up for a Christmas party in the winter of 2012 and I will fully admit that I cried. I had fallen in love with the parks and I will greatly attest that this was a big part of the driving force that pointed me towards Orlando.

"You know you can't just live in theme parks, right?" Rachel asked me one day while I was planning a vacation to the sunshine state. "Josh, you have to be an adult, you can't just live at Disney."

Challenge accepted.

Six months after that conversation and three years to the day after leaving my first comfort zone of the grocery store, I went big and found my entire life packed into my Honda Civic and embarking on an adventure. Twenty-four hours and two angry cats later, I settled into a brand new life in Orlando, Florida. It was a chance to hit the reset button in a way and try something new and completely terrifying.

Life in Orlando hasn't been all fun and games. Sure, I'm spoiled in that I can very much go to Walt Disney World and Universal Studios whenever I feel like it. I've made wonderful friends from inside the parks and from without. I was able to continue travelling to schools all over the county, not having to worry about winter storms grounding me in Boston. However, it would be a lie to say that it's all been perfect. It's really nothing that has to do with Florida but more what life has chosen to throw my way.

My relationship with Angus took a huge toll on me both emotionally and financially. I, without realizing it, was supporting him and paying his way and he ended up taking a lot of money from me. I was left in a hard spot financially because of him. Emotionally, I was a mess and lost focus on everything that was important to me. It was a dark and deeply embarrassing time for me and I struggled with great difficultly to move beyond what had happened to me.

Come 2016 the world was changing in some less than ideal ways. The political climate made educational institutions nervous and soon they were spending less and less on outside speakers and consultants. I took a job waiting tables to make ends meet. It felt like a huge step back in some ways but it was necessary to keep my head afloat. At the same time, it felt good in a way. Sure, I had made friends here and there around Orlando but nothing that was consistent. I had co-workers again, people to get to know and hang out with. It sounds almost childish to say out loud but it felt good to have friends again. Not only that but I had a new challenge of something I had never done before.

Here we are now. Nearly five years after taking a risk and moving my life over a thousand miles away from everything I knew and loved, I've found myself feeling that familiar itch again. 2019 marks my tenth year travelling and speaking at schools, a job that I truly love and can't get enough of. But there's that damn itch.

It's hard to say what the next ten years could possibly bring. Without knowing it I, long ago, placed myself on the road less travelled. I could have taken the path that was expected of me. I could have taken a job teaching and spent my years in a classroom as had been the plan way back when I first sent my application to Salem State. Or, what if I had never moved to Florida. Never met Angus, the man who damn near ruined me. I'd still have my job at the aquarium and my cozy little apartment.

Then I can't help but look around at all the things I wouldn't have. The friends I never would have met, the places I never would have seen, the pain I never would have felt, and the lessons I never would have learned. I would have missed out on the ride that has brought me to the place I am today. Hindsight is 20/20. Maybe the grass wasn't really greener on the other side but that doesn't mean you let the yard rot.

Life has managed to throw a lot at me in the past thirty-three years. I would be lying if I said I wouldn't go back and change a thing. I would love to be able to go back, even just five years with the knowledge that I have now. Even one year would be just fine by me, send me back and help me learn from the mistakes of this one year. Sadly, that's just not how life works.

What I can do, is take a long hard look at that one year, those five years, these past thirty-three years and learn from them.

When I first sat down, nearly ten years ago now, to begin writing this book I certainly had something a lot different in mind when it came to the final product. I also didn't think it was going to take me nearly ten years to write it so there's also that. I have, many times laughed and shrugged and commented I'm just doing it wrong. Maybe I'm not though. Who's to say that I'm doing anything wrong at all. Who's to say any of us are.

If I've learned anything from my time on this Earth, it's that everything happens for a reason. If there was anything that I learned from all of my time writing this book, it's that there is a lesson in everything. If we are willing and able to take the time to recognize and learn from what life throws at us, then we can grow and succeed. It's not always easy and it sometimes feels like the entire world is out to get you, but I promise, it's not.

There is no right or wrong answer when it comes to all of this, there really never has been. What worked for our parents doesn't work for us and truth is the same for their parents before them. Hell, I'm still trying to figure out what actually works for me. Maybe someday I'll find it in me to settle down, put down roots, have a family that doesn't consist of just cats. Maybe. Someday.

And there it is. After thirty-three years, ten of which spent writing a book, and five years in Florida, that itch is back. The one telling me that it's time for something new. Does that mean a new job? Does that mean moving to a new city? Does that mean adopting more cats? Very likely that last one. Doesn't matter too much because I'm going to keep doing my own thing.

And you? Here's my advice. Learn from everything the past is trying to tell you. Through thick and thin there is a lesson in every moment and you should listen to them. Stop defining yourself by your mistakes and thinking you can't move on. You are stronger because of them, you've learned because of them, and you've grown.

Me? Well, let's just hope I can finally learn to take my own advice.

thankful

I would really love to pretend that writing a book is the easiest thing in the entire world and was a completely solo effort but that would be the biggest lie ever. There are so many people who were instrumental in making this whole thing come to life. So many that I'm almost positive that I'm going to forget to thank someone here and feel like a jerk about it. So if I forget you, know that it's not personal and I feel terrible about it. Honestly, I've probably lost the most sleep over writing this because I feel like I need to list everyone I've ever known but then I risk this becoming one of those insane yearbook shout-out blurbs. And I'm not that popular.

I'm beyond grateful for my friend Nina Sabettini who allowed the idea for this book to come to life in her office during a lunch break and for years now has harassed me to get this thing done. She has been my biggest champion and still puts up with me despite the fact that I once called her on her birthday and failed to actually wish her a happy birthday. This is what happens when you wave an Italian beekeeper in my face. You really should have seen that coming.

Kevin Mori who has been my unwitting sounding board since we first met on Main Street, USA in Magic Kingdom. Thank you for the 4am texts, for not judging my mental breakdowns, for being there for me when I was digging deep into memories I would have really rather forgotten. Thank you for being there through thick and thin whether it's Thanksgiving dinner on another planet or forcing me to participate fully in the Festival of the Lion King.

My fake wife Ashley-Michelle Cole who has been my partner in adventure and who holds the record of longest Snapchat streak among my friends (she would feel it's important for the world to know this). Thank you for fueling my ego and not for not judging me that one time I drunkenly won Harry Potter trivia on a cruise ship and proceeded to rub my medal in everyone's face. That's right, I won a medal for Harry Potter trivia. Bow to me.

To Marsha "Mimi" Hughes for being the most loving and supportive human being I've ever met. I'm so grateful for you and how much joy you bring to my world. Our chances to catch up are few and far between but know that I cherish each and every one of them.

Thank you to my amazing friends who have supported me though all of this and so much more: Leslie Kay, Monica & Ryan Poulin, Melanie Strassheimer, Cat Cutenese, Casey Maute, Meg Pal (#NotYourBooHole #ThatsMyBarrel), Maggie Irvine, Tony Rossi, Bobby

Savage, Carrie Wogaman, Mandy Mitchell, Becky Kozak, Kayla Marx, Erica Walke and Taylor Mohney. I know I'm not the easiest person in the world to be friends with but somehow you do it. Ya'll deserve a medal. Or booze. Or both.

Shout out to my Aquarium family who made life an adventure every day whether guests were threatening to feed me to fish or you adjusted my schedule so I could flirt with cute guys: Megan Anderson, Sam Herman, Meg Stone, Deb Bobek, Christine Rohror, Patrick Beckles, Rachael Cross, Della Grallert and Gigi Krain. I miss you all every day and love when we are able to catch up. Let's do dinner!

Lastly to my siblings: Shannon, Erik and Melinda for letting me write about them so long as I promised not to make it too embarrassing. I'm saving that all for the next book so you're safe… for now.

JOSH GUNDERSON

about the author

See pages 1-254

www.avoidingneverland.com

Made in the USA
Columbia, SC
28 November 2020